QUICK AND EASY CHINESE COOKING

Kenneth Lo was born in Foochow, South China, and was educated at the Universities of Peking, Cambridge, and London. He was originally a student of physics, from which he changed to English Literature when he came to England. During his time in this country he has pursued a wide variety of careers and activities. He has been a diplomat, fine-art publisher, industrial relations and welfare officer (with Chinese seamen in Liverpool), journalist, lecturer, professional tennis player, and now food critic and cookery writer.

He has written many successful books on Chinese cookery. *Quick and Easy Chinese Cooking* became the Alternate choice of the Book of the Month Club for March 1972, and was further chosen by *Better Homes and Gardens Books* in their selection.

Apart from writing about Chinese cookery, he lectures widely on the subject, and talks and demonstrates occasionally on television. He has for several years been the Chinese food consultant to the Consumers' Association, and is at the moment adviser on Chinese food to several major food concerns both here and abroad.

Also available in Pan Books

ALL ABOUT COOKERY – Mrs Beeton
THE CONSTANCE SPRY COOKERY BOOK – Constance
Spry and Rosemary Hume
THE CORDON BLEU BOOK OF JAMS, PRESERVES AND
PICKLES – Rosemary Hume and Muriel Downes
MISS READ'S COUNTRY COOKING
DEEP-FREEZE COOKERY – Marika Hanbury Tenison
WORLD COOKERY – Marguerite Patten
LEARNING TO COOK – Marguerite Patten
HERBS FOR HEALTH AND COOKERY – Claire Loewenfeld
and Philippa Back
THE MARGARET POWELL COOKERY BOOK
THE POULTRY AND GAME COOK BOOK – Ruth Martin
SPANISH COOKING AT HOME AND ON HOLIDAY –
Marte Manjón and Catherine O'Brien

QUICK AND EASY CHINESE COOKING

KENNETH LO

REVISED EDITION

PAN BOOKS LTD : LONDON

First published 1970 by Pelham Books Ltd
This revised edition published 1973 by Pan Books Ltd,
33 Tothill Street, London SW1

ISBN 0 330 23707 1

*Printed and bound in England by
Hazell Watson & Viney Ltd,
Aylesbury, Bucks*

Contents

International Conversion Tables

These conversion tables are intended to help all users of Pan cookery books – wherever they live in the world. The weights and measures used throughout this book are based on British Imperial standards and metric units. However, the following tables show you how to convert the various weights and measures simply.

International Measures

Measure	UK	Australia	New Zealand	Canada
1 pint	20 fl oz	20 fl oz	20 fl oz	20 fl oz
1 cup	10 fl oz	8 fl oz	8 fl oz	8 fl oz
1 tablespoon	$\frac{5}{8}$ fl oz	$\frac{1}{2}$ fl oz	$\frac{1}{2}$ fl oz	$\frac{1}{2}$ fl oz
1 teaspoon	$\frac{1}{5}$ fl oz	$\frac{1}{8}$ fl oz	$\frac{1}{6}$ fl oz	$\frac{1}{6}$ fl oz

Conversion of fluid ounces to metric

35 fl oz (approx $1\frac{3}{4}$ Imperial pints)	= 1 litre (1000 millilitres or 10 decilitres)
1 Imperial pint (20 fl oz)	= approx 600 ml (6 dl)
$\frac{1}{2}$ Imperial pint (10 fl oz)	= 300 ml (3 dl)
$\frac{1}{4}$ Imperial pint (5 fl oz)	= 150 ml ($1\frac{1}{2}$ dl)
4 tablespoons ($2\frac{1}{2}$ fl oz)	= 70 ml (7 centilitres)
2 tablespoons ($1\frac{1}{4}$ fl oz)	= 35 ml ($3\frac{1}{2}$ cl)

1 tablespoon ($\frac{5}{8}$ fl oz)   = 18 ml (2 cl)
1 teaspoon ($\frac{1}{8}$ fl oz)   = 6 ml

(All the above metric equivalents are approximate)

Conversion of solid weights to metric

2 lb 3 oz = 1 k (kilogram)
1 lb   = 453 gm (grammes)
12 oz   = 339 gm
8 oz   = 225 gm
4 oz   = 113 gm
2 oz   = 56 gm
1 oz   = 28 gm

Equivalents

I UK (old BSI standard) cup equals 1$\frac{1}{4}$ cups in
Commonwealth countries
4 UK tablespoons equal 5 Commonwealth tablespoons
5 UK teaspoons equal 6 New Zealand or 6 Canada or
8 Australia

In British cookery books, a gill is usually 5 fl oz ($\frac{1}{4}$ pint), but
in a few localities in the UK it can mean 10 fl oz ($\frac{1}{2}$ pint).

Other non-standardized measures include:
Breakfast cup = approx 10 fl oz
Tea cup   = 6 fl oz
Coffee cup   = 3 fl oz

Oven temperatures

Description	Electric Setting	Gas Mark
Very cool	225°F (110°C)	$\frac{1}{4}$
	250°F (130°C)	$\frac{1}{2}$
Cool	275°F (140°C)	1
	300°F (150°C)	2
Very moderate	325°F (170°C)	3
Moderate	350°F (180°C)	4

Description	Electric Setting	Gas Mark
Moderately or	375°F (190°C)	5
fairly hot	400°F (200°C)	6
Hot	425°F (220°C)	7
	450°F (230°C)	8
Very hot	475°F (240°C)	9

These temperatures are only an approximate guide as all ovens vary slightly, according to the make and country of manufacture.

Foreword

All the recipes in this book are either quick or easy to cook, or both.

Those which cook rapidly are all quite simple to prepare, and most of those which require longer cooking take almost no time to assemble and practically cook themselves. For this reason, we Chinese invariably include one or two long-cooked dishes in planning our meals. In this way, by reducing the number of things one has to do at a given time, a multi-dish dinner can be tackled with relative ease. Once you have achieved the rhythm of preparing a Chinese meal at a measured and leisurely pace, you have more than half won the battle – if it can be so described!

Although some excellent Chinese cookery books have been published in recent years, many of them stress authenticity and atmosphere so heavily that they have inadvertently contributed to the mystique surrounding this subject. By reducing the process of Chinese cooking to something which can be both *quick* and *easy*, I hope that the contents of this book will help dispel something of this mystique. After all, anything which can be done both quickly and easily, from quite ordinary materials and ingredients, cannot be too mystical! (Anybody who has examined at close quarters the foods and dishes prepared in the Imperial Palace Kitchens of the Forbidden City would hardly argue this point.)

Many of the dishes in this book require no more than 4–5

minutes of preparation and 3–4 minutes' cooking time. Those which require longer cooking often need no more than 1–2 minutes to prepare, and are, therefore, even less time-consuming. I hope that these dishes – undemanding as most of them are – will tempt the reader to try his hand at a style of cuisine which can honestly be described as fun, and which is at the same time highly varied, nutritional and extremely tasty.

Kenneth Lo

Introduction

Basic Ingredients

Many people have the impression that it is necessary to use a great many rare and exotic ingredients in Chinese cooking. This is not so at all. The basic food-materials are for all practical purposes the same as those used in Western cooking.

As for flavouring and seasoning, so long as you have soya sauce – which is obtainable almost anywhere these days – you can cook Chinese. Almost all the other seasoning ingredients are precisely the same as those we normally use: salt, pepper, chilli powder, mustard, parsley, chives, garlic, onion and spring onions. And in most recipes, one or two teaspoons of finely sliced onion can be used in place of spring onions when they are out of season.

Substitutions can also be used for the one or two more exotic ingredients. For example, root ginger can be replaced by finely chopped lemon rind shavings – but *seldom* by powdered ginger. Fresh mushrooms can be used in place of dried ones; if available, however, dried mushrooms are certainly preferable. (They are always soaked in a little hot water for 20–30 minutes, and then de-stemmed before using.)

There are a few western ingredients and seasonings which would be useful to have around when you intend to cook Chinese:

cornflour,
dry sherry,
chilli sauce (tabasco),
tomato sauce (ketchup) or tomato purée,
gelatine powder,
mustard,
pickles and chutneys.

If convenience foods or frozen foods are admissible in good western cooking, they can certainly also be incorporated into good Chinese cooking, provided they are pepped up with a proportion of fresh foods at crucial points in the process.

Kitchen Equipment and Utensils

It is often supposed that to practise Chinese cooking one would require a whole range of Chinese equipment and kitchen utensils. Not at all. One can cook Chinese without the use of any of the typically Chinese equipment. I have done so for years. The equipment of a modern kitchen is quite capable of coping with all forms and styles of Chinese cooking, and may indeed have many advantages over the typical Chinese kitchen. This is not to say that there are not some items in use in the Chinese kitchen which are immensely effective. The razor-sharp chopper, the half-foot-thick tree-trunk chopping board, the round-bottomed smooth-contoured frying-pan (the *wok*) and the multi-layer bamboo basket steamer all have their strong points, but unless you are already well-practised in their uses, their presence would contribute more to the rustic effect than to general efficiency.

The only things you really need to start cooking Chinese in your kitchen are simply a couple of saucepans and frying-pans, and a good long-handled metal spoon for stir-frying.

It would be an advantage to have a frying-pan which is equipped with a lid, for, when you introduce wet materials into a pan with very hot oil, you may need to shield yourself from the consequent spattering! And also, in Chinese 'stir-frying', you often introduce a few spoonfuls of broth, and close the lid for a couple of minutes of braising under cover, before restarting another session of final stir-fry. As for saucepans, it would be useful to possess at least one heavy one, or an iron pot, which can be used for long-simmering. The wide range of heavy casseroles which are currently available should come in handy, both for cooking on the range and for long-simmering in the oven.

One type of cooking which is practised more widely in China than in the West is steaming. It would be useful, therefore, to have a steamer, particularly an oval-shaped or an elongated one, so that a whole fish can be cooked in it. Lacking this, one can always convert any large saucepan into a steamer simply by placing food to be cooked in a deep-sided heatproof dish (or basin) and standing it in a saucepan surrounded by about one inch of water. When the water is brought to the boil the food in the dish or basin will be steamed as if in a steamer. The only thing one has to be careful about is not to allow any of the water in the pan to slosh into the dish containing the food. When a comparatively shallow heatproof dish is used, the dish will have to be placed on a platform above the boiling water. This can be achieved by placing two or three china or metal egg-cups at the bottom of the pan. In the case of 'long-steaming', the dish containing the food is usually closed. This 'closed steaming' is really equivalent to double-boiling and can in fact be done in a double-boiler.

You will not require anything aside from this basic equipment, although it would be useful to have a collection of bowls, saucers and small dishes into which you can place the various ingredients and cut-up materials when preparing food for cooking.

Although there are at least 49 established methods of cooking in Chinese cuisine, the only method which a westerner will have to learn is 'stir-frying' (sometimes known as 'quick-frying,' or – to give a graphic description of what actually happens –

'quick-stir-frying'). Of the other 48 methods, many are in common use in the west – deep-frying, grilling, roasting, etc. The bulk of them are preoccupied with delicate operations of controlled acceleration and deceleration of heating (such as cooking in 'receding heat', or by rapid reduction of liquid), or more or less use of water, wine or oil, at different stages of heating. I do not feel that preoccupation with these fancy methods, no matter how time-honoured and established, will add much to one's initial mastery of Chinese cooking. Learning the technique of stir-frying, however, is a must.

Stir-frying

Stir-frying is in its essence very simple. It involves heating a small quantity of oil or fat (usually not much more than 2–3 tablespoons) in a frying-pan or saucepan – the latter splashes less. When the oil becomes very hot, as it does within seconds, the meat or other ingredients are added and stirred together. The stirring is simply the action of stirring, turning, scrambling, and occasionally tossing (here one has to be careful) the food so that all parts of it are evenly covered in hot oil and their contact with the hot pan is rotated and evenly maintained. This assures that the food is quickly and evenly done.

The food-materials used have generally been cut into very thin slices, or shredded into matchstick-thin strips, or diced into $\frac{1}{4}$- to $\frac{3}{4}$-inch cubelets. They are stirred in the hot oil for a few seconds to 3–4 minutes, with a metal spoon or bamboo chopsticks, then they are removed and put aside. A further small quantity of oil (about 1 tablespoon) is usually added to the pan, followed by the other constituents of the dish – often dried or fresh vegetables (also cut up into thin slices, shreds, or small cubes) – for a short period of frying (a few seconds to 2 minutes). In the final phase the meat is again returned into the pan for a final 'assembly frying' with all the other materials.

This final stir-frying generally does not last for more than a minute. Often at this stage a small amount of chicken broth and wine or sherry is added to prevent scorching and provide some gravy for the dish. Seasonings can often be adjusted at this point, and not infrequently cornflour (blended in triple its amount of water) is added, especially when there is ample gravy. In some instances a drop or two of aromatic oil (such as sesame oil) stirred in at the last moment will add to the fragrance of the dish. (In the West a drop or two of liqueur might help add aromatic appeal.)

When cooking vegetables and seafoods, a small amount of chopped onion (spring onions), garlic and root ginger (where available) are usually introduced and fried in hot oil for a $\frac{1}{4}$ to $\frac{1}{2}$ minute before the other ingredients are added. By impregnating the oil first with these strong-flavoured vegetables, and then lubricating the main foods with it, the appeal of the dish is often heightened and any over-fishiness or other unwanted taste or smell is suppressed.

It should be noted that, when food-materials are cut into very small or thin pieces, under the action of very hot oil, even pork can be well-cooked within 3-4 minutes. Beef and chicken can often be cooked in under half a minute (depending partly on quantity of food and size of pan), and soft vegetables in 1-2 minutes. If anything is suspected of being slightly under-cooked, adjustment can usually be made in the final 'assembly frying'. Quite often foods will cook to some extent in their own heat while awaiting this final session of cooking. There is plenty of room for adjustments in all the various stages of the procedure, and this is what makes Chinese cooking so flexible.

When all the actions are carried out with rapidity and rhythm, stir-frying is rather like conducting an orchestra. The chef orchestrates the flavours and heat and demonstrates his virtuosity, aiming for balance, harmony and impact.

Timing

Individual Chinese dishes can often be prepared and cooked very quickly – in a matter of a few minutes. But a proper Chinese meal is a communal meal, cooked and served for the whole family, or a group of at least 3-4 people. Such a meal should consist of a minimum of 3-4 dishes, in addition to rice and soup. Because of this multiplicity of dishes, a Chinese meal will consume some time to prepare and cook.

Two things greatly reduce time in Chinese cooking: the practice of cooking several dishes at the same time – a habit which comes more easily and naturally than you would imagine – and the habit of having all the necessary foods and made-up ingredients ready before-hand. Both of these habits are ingrained in Chinese cooks. For westerners who are initiates to the practice of Chinese cooking these two points should be continually kept in mind.

If one were to start from scratch, without any of the foods and ingredients prepared or made up, a meal of three dishes with soup and rice, might require an hour or more to prepare. But if some of the foods can be prepared at moments of leisure, and some of the ingredients made up and laid out before-hand, and if, wherever possible, the dishes are cooked simultaneously, the time required can be easily reduced by half.

In a professional Chinese kitchen, where everything is on hand, one often sees dishes cooked in two or three minutes. And occasionally, when several frying-pans are working at feverish speed at the same time, it is possible for the speed to rise to the incredible rate of four dishes a minute! But with us ordinary mortals, who should be content with producing a dish in 10–15 minutes, the time required for preparing and cooking a meal of soup, rice and three other dishes may well be kept to under 30 minutes by anyone who has had a couple of run-throughs of the procedure.

For instance, in preparing such a meal, the rice and soup can usually be started off first on the two back burners, leaving the two front burners for cooking the meat dish and vegetable dish, while the oven can be used to cook the third savoury dish. Here one simply has to calculate it so that all the dishes will be ready at the same time – just as one does for a traditional roast dinner.

By the time you have got the soup and rice started, and the third dish in the oven, you will only have the meat dish and vegetable dish to deal with. Since vegetables seldom take more than 5 minutes to cook, and meat which has been sliced, shredded, or diced needs no more than 6–7 minutes, it should take 15 minutes to cook these two dishes separately and only 10 minutes if you do them simultaneously, so you should have plenty of time in hand. In fact, you should be able to cook them at leisure.

'Shredded' Meats and Vegetables

In Chinese cooking, foods which are finely sliced into thin strips are commonly referred to as 'shredded'. On no account should this term be interpreted to require the use of a metal grater or shredder. To shred anything in the Chinese manner, one simply uses a sharp knife to cut the food along the grain into 1- or 2-inch-length strips that are about twice the width of a matchstick.

Menu-making and Portions

In planning a Chinese meal it is best to regard it as a buffet, where everybody helps himself from the spread of dishes on the table. As such, there should be at least three or four dishes for the diners to help themselves from. As a rule a Chinese meal of three or four dishes is meant to serve three or four persons. Should the number of diners increase by one or two, it is not always necessary to increase the number of dishes accordingly. If one or two of them are large dishes, as they often are, there should easily be sufficient food for everyone.

Most Chinese long-cooked dishes of meat stew and poultry are substantial dishes which, if not completely consumed in one meal, can easily be heated up again for another. When these are supplemented by one or two quick-cooked dishes (usually stir-fried ones), plus a soup and rice, you have a complete, well-balanced Chinese meal. The soup, by the way, is treated as one item of the buffet and is left on the table to be drunk a mouthful or two at a time throughout the meal – in place of water or any other beverage.

What is a well-balanced Chinese menu? It is simply a menu with items which represent a good variety in materials, colour and texture. For example, if you have a heavy, long-cooked meat dish, you will have a pure vegetable dish to balance it, the vegetable being green, fresh and crunchy, the meat being brown, rich and tender. Further to balance the meal, you may have a fish or other seafood dish or boiled chicken or an egg dish, the egg being yellow, the fish and chicken white, the sea-food pink.

Since the majority of Chinese meat or vegetable dishes are capable of numerous minor variations, there is never any lack of items to fill up the gap, depending on what is at hand. Then again, of course, the choice depends upon one's inclination: if you are inclined towards seafood, you can have a seafood dish in addition to a fish dish; and if you are inclined towards meat, you can have a quick-fried meat dish in addition to the main 'stewed' meat dish. The choice of quick-fried meat and vegetable dishes is extremely varied, and depends only on matching the vegetables or other ingredients with meat which has been rendered particularly suitable to their size and shape: minced meat with peas, shredded meats with shredded vegetables, large pieces of chopped meat with carrots or turnips and diced meats with nuts. The possibilities here are quite limitless.

Portions: The recipes in this book are basically calculated for 4 portions, to be placed on the table along with 3 other dishes. There will be instances where there will be more food than can be consumed. In such cases, the leftovers should be kept in a refrigerator to be reheated and rearranged for another meal. To do this is very much in the tradition of Chinese cooking and eating.

Suggested Menus

Here are four lots of suggested menus, oriented towards *meat, poultry, fish and other seafood* and *vegetables*.

For those westerners who intend to cook something simple for themselves or for just two people, the best plan would be to stick to the rice and noodle dishes (Fried Rice, Topped Rice and Noodles) and to cook just one other dish – of a contrasting material. If the rice or noodles are topped or fried with pork, cook a seafood or chicken and mushroom dish to go along with it. To cater to such requirements, I have provided a fifth set of menus, 'Extra Quick and Easy Menus'.

It will be noted that plain boiled rice is eaten with the dishes of the first four types of menu; it is there to absorb some of the richness and provide the bulk. In the case of the fifth category, noodles or rice appear as the main constituent of one dish in a two-dish combination, so there is no necessity of providing any other bland food to offset what might have been over-savouriness. Soup is provided in all menus except the 'Extra Quick and Easy' ones.

I have given only a very limited number of sweets in this book, mainly because it is not the Chinese custom to serve desserts at mealtime. The four desserts at the end of the book and their possible variants will fit most menus; alternatively, any of the lighter western desserts can be used to conclude a Chinese meal.

And for the types of wines to drink with Chinese meals? Chinese wines are as yet too difficult to obtain. The best western wines to drink with Chinese meals are all the light, dry, white wines – nothing sweet or heavy, since most Chinese savoury dishes already contain some elements of sugar. A sparkling wine is suitable for starting off a Chinese meal where hors d'oeuvres are served.

Meat-orientated

(All the following menus are meant for 4–6 people)

Menu 1
Spare-rib and Cucumber Soup (see pp.23–4)
Red-cooked Pork (see pp.57–8)
Quick-fried Sliced Beef with Oysters (see pp.77–8)
Plain-fried Spinach (see p.165)
Steamed Eggs (see p.122)
Boiled Rice (see pp.35–6)

Menu 2
Lamb and Leek Soup (see pp.28–9)
Quick-fried Ribbons of Beef with Bean-sprouts (see pp.73–4)
White-cooked Pork (see p.61)

Triple-layer Scrambled-omelette (see pp.118–19)
Red-cooked Cabbage (see pp.167–8)
Boiled Rice (see pp.35–6)

Menu 3
Sliced Beef with Tomato and Egg-flower Soup (see p.26)
Triple-quick-fries (see pp.82–3)
Red-cooked Spare-ribs (see p.60)
Egg-flower Meat (see pp.120–21)
Quick-fried White-braised Cauliflower (see pp.170–71)
Boiled Rice (see pp.35–6)

Menu 4
Sliced Pork and Mushroom Soup (see p.27)
Red-cooked Beef (see pp.78–9)
Quick-fried Sliced Lamb with Young Leeks (see p.81)
Scrambled-omelette with Sweet and Sour Sauce (see p.118)
Quick-fried Broccoli in Fu-yung Sauce (see pp.171–2)
Boiled Rice (see pp.35–6)

Poultry-orientated

(All the following menus are meant for 4–6 people)

Menu 1
Cream of Fish Soup with Shrimps (see p.31)
Red-cooked Chicken (Whole) (see p.101)
Orange Duck (see pp.113–14)
Vegetarian Scrambled-omelette (see p.120)
Quick-fried Braised Lettuce (see p.172)
Boiled Rice (see pp.35–6)

Menu 2
Sliced Beef with Watercress Soup (see p.25)
Diced Chicken Quick-fried in Soya Sauce (see p.87)
Aromatic and Crispy Duck (see p.107)
Chinese Salad (see p.176)
Boiled Rice (see pp.35–6)

Menu 3
Pork Spare-ribs and Celery Soup (see p.24)
Chopped, Salted Deep-fried Chicken (see pp.93–4)
Pan-roast, Red-cooked Duck (see p.108)
Stir-fried Shredded Pork with Spring Onions (see pp.66–7)
Red-cooked Celery (see p.170)
Boiled Rice (see pp.35–6)

Menu 4
White Fish and Green Pea Soup (see p.30)
Diced Chicken Quick-fried in 'Hot Sauce' (see p.88)
Clear-simmered Duck with Onion and Spring Greens (see pp.
110–11)
Quick-fried Shrimps with Mushrooms in Gunpowder Sauce
(see pp.152–3)
Steamed 'Vegetable Bowl' (see p.175)
Boiled Rice (see pp.35–6)

Fish- and Seafood-orientated

(All the following menus are meant for 4–6 people)

Menu 1
Chinese Chicken Noodle Soup (see pp.32–3)
Red-cooked Fish (see p.125)
Abalone Quick-fried with Mushrooms and Broccoli (see pp.
142–3)
Stuffed Sweet Peppers (see pp.70–71)
Casserole of Cabbage and Brussels Sprouts with Pig's Trotters
(see pp.173–4)

Menu 2
White Fish and Spring Green Soup (see pp.30–31)
Plain Salted Double-fried Fish Steaks (see pp.128–9)
Quick-fried Giant Prawns with Tomatoes (see pp.151–2)
Minced Pork 'Pudding' with Cauliflower (see p.70)
Boiled Rice (see pp.35–6)

Menu 3
Lamb and Leek Soup (see pp.28–9)
Sweet and Sour Carp (see p.127)
Quick-fried Crabs in Egg Sauce (see p.146)
Stir-fried Sliced Pork with Cabbage (see p.69)
Boiled Rice (see pp.35–6)

Menu 4
'Triple-shred' Soup (see p.28)
Grilled Crabs (see pp.147–8)
Clear-simmered Fish (see p.131)
Drunken Duck (see pp.109–10)
Casserole of Leeks and Cabbage with Lamb Chops (see pp.174–5)
Boiled Rice (see pp.35–6)

Vegetable-orientated

(All the following menus are meant for 4–6 people)

Menu 1
Vegetable Soup (see p.34)
Plain Fried Spinach (see p.165)
Red-cooked Cabbage (see pp.167–8)
Crab Scrambled-omelette (see p.119)
Fish Steaks in Sweet and Sour Sauce (see p.129)
Diced Chicken with Sweet Pepper and Chilli Pepper (see pp.88–9)
Boiled Rice (see pp.35–6)

Menu 2
'Soup of the Gods' (see p.34)
White-cooked Celery (see p.170)
Casserole of Cabbage and Brussels Sprouts with Squabs (see p.174)
Plain Salted Double-fried Fish Steaks (see pp.128–9)
Soya-simmered Hard-boiled Eggs (see pp.121–2)
Boiled Rice (see pp.35–6)

Menu 3
Green Jade Soup (see p.33)
Red-cooked Celery (see p.170)
Stir-fried Spinach with Shrimps (see p.165)
Red-cooked Fish Steaks (see pp.127-8)
Chopped Braised-fried Chicken in Wine Sediment Paste (see p.95)
Boiled Rice (see pp.35-6)

Menu 4
Green and White Soup (see p.29)
White-cooked Cabbage (see p.168)
Quick-fried Sweet Pepper with Shredded Beef (see pp.172-3)
Double-fried Eel (see p.133)
Fancy Steamed Eggs (see p.123)
Boiled Rice (see pp.35-6)

Extra Quick and Easy Menus

To have a really quickly prepared Chinese meal, one has to re-sort to rice and noodles dishes. The following section of two-dish combinations are meant for small families, bed-sitter dwellers or anyone who wishes to prepare a quick, tasty meal with a minimum of fuss. All the menus are meant for 1-2 persons, depending upon the appetite and capacity of the people concerned. As no soup is provided, these dishes may be accompanied by beer, tea or coffee.

RICE
Meal 1
Meat Fried Rice (see p.37)
Quick-fried Sliced Lamb with Young Leeks (see p.81)

Meal 2
Fried Rice with Seafood (see pp.38-9)
Diced Chicken Quick-fried in Soya Sauce (see p.87)

Meal 3
Vegetable Fried Rice (see pp.36–7)
Red-cooked Fish Steaks (see pp.127–8)

Meal 4
'Topped Rice' with Diced Chicken, Shrimps and Green Peas (see p.40)
Quick-fried Giant Prawns with Tomatoes (see pp.151–2)

Meal 5
'Topped Rice' with Sweet and Sour Pork and Fu-yung Cauliflower (see pp.40–41)
Stir-fried Spinach with Shrimps (see p.165)

Meal 6
'Topped Rice' with Sliced Soya Steak and Broccoli (see pp.39–40)
Egg-flower Meat (see pp.120–21)

NOODLES
Meal 1
Chicken and Mushroom Chow Mein with French Beans (see pp.43–4)
Quick-fried Sliced Beef with Kidney (see pp.76–7)

Meal 2
Lamb and Leek Chow Mein (see p.45)
Stir-fried Pork with Bean-sprouts (see p.66)

Meal 3
Chow Mein with Shredded Duck Meat and Celery (see p.47)
Diced Chicken Quick-fried with Cucumber and Button Mushrooms (see pp.89–90)

Meal 4
Gravy Noodles with Red-cooked Pork and Spinach (see p.48)
Shredded Chicken Quick-fried with Bean-sprouts (see p.103)

Meal 5
Gravy Noodles with Spiced Beef and Tomatoes (see p.49)
Sliced Chicken Quick-fried with Pig's Liver (see pp.92–3)

Meal 6
Gravy Noodles with Chicken and Oyster (see pp.49–50)
Triple-quick-fries with Wine Sediment Paste (see p.83)

Broths and Sauces

Chinese cooking can be made even quicker and easier if a few basic composite materials, commonly used in Chinese cooking, are made up beforehand, so that they can be taken from the store-cupboard or refrigerator for use whenever required. There are only a few of these made-up materials, and they are prepared from ingredients which are available everywhere today. They are:

Superior Broth.
'Gunpowder Sauce' (this is what we Chinese use in almost every other dish).
Fu-yung White Sauce.
Sweet and Sour Sauce.
Wine Sediment Paste.

SUPERIOR BROTH

The Chinese 'superior broth', which we shall for convenience just call 'broth', is used in nearly all non-meat dishes (including soup), and accounts for the tastiness and savouriness of much Chinese food. Although it is traditionally made with pork ribs, a meaty chicken carcass and a small portion of chicken meat, the chicken can be eliminated if necessary, and belly of pork can be substituted for the ribs – providing one is careful to skim off all the fat when the broth is cold. The following recipe will yield 2–2½ pints, which should be more than ample for a large Chinese meal (including soup).

1 lb pork spare-ribs (or belly of pork) 1 meaty chicken carcass and a small piece chicken (optional)	2½ pints water 1 chicken stock cube (add an extra ½ cube if not using chicken)

Simmer the meat in the water for about 1 hour. Add the stock cube(s) and simmer for a further 20 minutes. Set aside until cold; then skim the surface and remove the meat and bones. (It is essential to leave the stock until it is completely cold in order to remove all the fat and impurities.)

The broth can be stored in the refrigerator for several days, and any excess can be added to soups.

QUICK SUBSTITUTE 'BROTH'

Since only a few tablespoons of broth are required in most of the recipes (excluding soups), a small piece of a chicken stock cube can be used, mixed into a little water, to provide a quick substitute.

GUNPOWDER SAUCE

I call this 'gunpowder sauce' because it is the sauce which is chiefly responsible for the difference between Chinese and western cooking. Except for the plain-cooked and white-cooked dishes, it is used in nearly all meat, poultry, fish and vegetable dishes. Normally one does not use a great quantity of it (in fried dishes seldom more than 2–3 tablespoons), but it will be handy to keep at least half a pint of it on hand:

½ pint soya sauce
6 tablespoons sherry
6 tablespoons 'broth'
1 tablespoon sugar
3 slices root ginger (or

finely chopped lemon rind
shavings)
1½ tablespoons chopped
onion
½ chicken stock cube

Heat and simmer the above ingredients together for fifteen minutes, stirring occasionally. Keep in the refrigerator.

FU-YUNG WHITE SAUCE

The principal difference between Chinese and western white sauce lies in the western use of milk, flour and butter, and the Chinese use of egg white, minced chicken and broth (occasionally with white wine thrown in). If we could use both types of ingredients, we would have the best of both worlds. And why not? The best way to make this is probably as follows:

3 tablespoons butter
4 tablespoons flour
6 tablespoons 'broth'
½ cup milk
4 tablespoons finely minced
chicken (optional)

2 egg whites
½ teaspoon salt
pepper (to taste)
3 tablespoons cream (or
unsweetened evaporated
milk)

Heat butter and make a roux with the flour, as you normally do in making a white sauce. Slowly pour in 'broth' and milk, stirring all the time. When that is well blended, add the chicken (if used), egg whites (beaten until almost stiff), salt and pepper. Continue to stir, and finally add the cream (or evaporated milk). Stir until the white sauce is smooth.

This sauce can be used successfully with vegetables (such as cauliflower), which have been pre-fried, or braised or cooked in 'broth'. It is often used with chicken (boiled, long-simmered and sliced), or in mixtures of sea-foods and diced chicken (in which case a small amount of white wine should be added).

It is best used fresh but can be kept in the refrigerator for a day or two.

SWEET AND SOUR SAUCE

This sauce is often made as required, since it takes up very little time, is simplicity itself to make, and is best used fresh. Most often used on meat and fish, and sometimes on vegetables, it is occasionally pepped up by adding a small amount of chilli sauce or dried chilli pepper. The following recipe will yield 6–8 tablespoons or approximately ½ cup of sauce.

1 tablespoon sugar
½ tablespoon cornflour, blended in 2 tablespoons water
1 tablespoon vinegar
1 tablespoon tomato purée
1 tablespoon orange (or pineapple) juice

1 tablespoon soya sauce
1 tablespoon sherry
½ red or green pepper (optional)
1 tablespoon pickles
2 tablespoons oil (use 1 teaspoon if omitting the pepper)

Mix first 7 ingredients in a bowl. Cut sweet pepper into thin slices, and chop pickles. Heat oil in a saucepan or frying pan. When hot add the pickles and sweet pepper (if used) to stir-fry slowly together for 1 minute. Pour in the sauce mixture, and stir until the sauce thickens, when it will be ready for use.

WINE SEDIMENT PASTE

In China 'Wine Sediment Paste' is made from the lees or dregs from the bottom of wine jars. It is used with great success in cooking with meats, poultry, fish and seafood. A version of it can be made by simply mixing together the following ingredients.

2 tablespoons tomato purée
1 tablespoon soya sauce

1 tablespoon sherry
3 teaspoons brandy

This is very winey material. When it is applied to lightly cooked foods such as boiled chicken or fish, it gives them a 'drunken' effect, and preserves them for long periods of time if kept in sealed jars.

SALT-AND-PEPPER MIX

This mix is an ideal accompaniment to various deep-fried chicken and fish dishes and is simplicity itself to prepare. The following amount should be enough to serve 3–4 diners.

2 tablespoons salt   2 teaspoons pepper

Heat salt and pepper in a dry pan over moderate heat for 1 minute, and place in small saucers to be set on the table along with saucers of tomato ketchup.

Soups

Portions: All the following recipes are meant to serve 4–6 people.

'Broth' (see recipe on pp.18–19) is an essential constituent of Chinese soups. Indeed, it is the base of nearly all, whether they be meat, vegetables, fish or 'combination' soups. In preparing soups I must presume that the 'broth' is already made.

PORK SPARE-RIBS AND CUCUMBER SOUP

PREPARATION TIME: 5–6 minutes. COOKING TIME: 55 minutes.

1 lb spare-ribs	1 pint 'broth' (see pp.18–19)
1 6-inch segment of a	1 teaspoon salt
large-size cucumber	pepper
(scraped but not peeled)	½ tablespoon soya sauce

Cut spare-ribs into individual ribs. Trim away any uneven or fatty bits. Place in 1 pint of water. Bring to boil, and simmer for 40 minutes. Pour off half the water and skim away any impurities.

Cut cucumber into three 2-inch segments, and then cut each segment lengthwise into 8 strips. Add them to the saucepan, together with 'broth', salt and pepper. Simmer together for 15 minutes, add soya sauce, and serve in a large tureen (for diners to help themselves from) or in individual bowls. (Diners should be encouraged to pick up the ribs and chew them, after drinking the soup.)

PORK SPARE-RIBS AND CELERY SOUP

PREPARATION TIME: 5–6 minutes. COOKING TIME: 50–55 minutes.

Follow the previous recipe, using 3 large stalks of celery instead of cucumber. As with cucumber, add the celery to the soup approximately 15 minutes before serving.

PORK SPARE-RIBS WITH CARROT AND TURNIP SOUP

PREPARATION TIME: 5–6 minutes. COOKING TIME: 65 minutes.

1 lb spare-ribs	1 pint 'broth' (see pp.18–19)
½–¾ lb bacon bones	1 teaspoon salt
¼ lb carrots	pepper to taste
¼ lb turnips	

Prepare the spare-ribs as in the first recipe. Boil them with the bacon bones in 1½ pints of water for 30 minutes, then pour away half the water (with the impurities) and remove bacon bones.

Peel and cut away any coarse parts of the vegetables and cut them into triangular wedge-shaped pieces. Add them to the spare-ribs, together with the 'broth'. Adjust the seasonings, simmer for 35 minutes and serve.

Longer cooking time is required in this case to soften the hard vegetables as well as to tenderize the spare-ribs.

BEEF WITH CUCUMBER AND CELERY SOUP

PREPARATION TIME: 5–6 minutes. COOKING TIME: 1 hour 50 minutes.

1 lb beef (shin, flank or stewing steak)	¼ lb celery
¼ lb cucumber (scraped but not peeled)	1 pint 'broth' (see pp.18–19)
	1 teaspoon salt
	pepper

Simmer the beef in 1½ pints water for 20 minutes. Skim and pour away a quarter of the water. Simmer very gently for 1 hour.

Cut cucumber and celery into strips. Add to the stock, along with the 'broth'. Simmer together for another 30 minutes, adjust for seasonings, and serve.

SLICED BEEF WITH WATERCRESS SOUP

PREPARATION TIME: 4–5 minutes. COOKING TIME: 5–6 minutes.

¼ lb beef steak (rump or fillet)	1 bundle watercress
2 teaspoons cornflour	1½ pints 'broth' (see pp.18–19)
1 teaspoon salt	pepper

Cut beef with sharp knife into 1-inch × ½-inch paper-thin slices. Rub with cornflour and half the salt. Clean watercress thoroughly, removing some of the muddier roots.

Heat 'broth' in a saucepan. Soon after boiling add beef and watercress to simmer in the 'broth' for 4–5 minutes. Adjust the seasonings and serve.

SLICED BEEF WITH TOMATO
AND EGG-FLOWER SOUP

PREPARATION TIME: 3–4 minutes. COOKING TIME: 7–8 minutes.

¼ lb beef steak (rump or fillet)   cut into thin slices
1 teaspoon salt   1 egg
2 teaspoons cornflour   ½ tablespoon soya sauce
1¾ pints 'broth' (see pp.18–19)   pepper
3 medium-sized tomatoes,

Cut beef into 1-inch × ½-inch paper-thin slices. Rub with salt and cornflour. Heat 'broth' in a saucepan. Soon after boiling add tomato to simmer for 3 minutes. Add beef and simmer for a further 3 minutes. Beat egg for 10 seconds and stream it along the prongs of a fork slowly into the soup. Allow the egg 10 seconds to set. Add soya sauce, adjust the seasonings and serve.

BEEF AND ONION SOUP

PREPARATION TIME: 3–4 minutes. COOKING TIME: 1½ hours.

¾ lb stewing beef   pepper
3 large onions, thinly sliced   2 tablespoons sherry
1½ pints 'broth' (see pp.18–19)   (optional)
2 tablespoons soya sauce

Cut beef into 1-inch cubes, and boil it in 1 pint of water for 30 minutes. Skim for impurities and pour away a third of the water. Add onion, 'broth' and soya sauce. Simmer together for 1 hour. Adjust the seasonings. Add sherry (optional), simmer for a further minute and serve.

SLICED PORK AND MUSHROOM SOUP

PREPARATION TIME: 3–4 minutes. COOKING TIME: 10–12 minutes.

¼ lean pork	1¾ pints 'broth' (see pp. 18–19)
1 teaspoon salt	1 tablespoon soya sauce
2 teaspoons cornflour	1 tablespoon sherry
1 small can button mushrooms	pepper

Cut pork into thin 1-inch × ½-inch slices. Rub with salt and cornflour. Cut mushrooms vertically into thin slices. Heat broth in saucepan. When it starts to boil add pork. Simmer for 5 minutes. Add mushrooms and simmer for another 3 minutes. Add soya sauce, sherry and adjust the seasoning. Stir, simmer for another 2 minutes and serve.

SLICED PORK AND CELERY CABBAGE SOUP

PREPARATION TIME: 3–4 minutes. COOKING TIME: 14–15 minutes.

Follow the previous recipe, substituting ½ lb celery cabbage for the mushrooms. Shred the cabbage and heat with pork from the beginning.

If celery cabbage – also called Chinese cabbage – is not available, use celery or savoy cabbage.

SLICED PORK AND BEAN-SPROUT SOUP

PREPARATION TIME: 3–4 minutes. COOKING TIME: 5–6 minutes.

Follow the above recipe for Sliced Pork and Mushroom Soup, replacing the mushrooms with 1–1½ cups bean-sprouts. The sprouts will require no more than 2 minutes' simmering.

SLICED PORK AND BROCCOLI SOUP

PREPARATION TIME: 3–4 minutes. COOKING TIME: 9–10 minutes.

Follow the recipe for Sliced Pork and Mushroom Soup, substituting broccoli for mushrooms as follows: cut away the root and coarser parts of ¾ lb of broccoli. Slice into individual branches. Boil for 3 minutes. Pour away water, and add broccoli to simmering 'broth' with pork.

'TRIPLE-SHRED' SOUP

PREPARATION TIME: 3–4 minutes. COOKING TIME: 4–5 minutes.

1 chicken breast (see note on p.86)	abalone (cut ditto)
3 tablespoons shredded ham (cut into matchstick-sized strips)	½ teaspoon salt
	2 teaspoons cornflour
	1¾ pints 'broth' (see pp.18–19)
	2 tablespoons sherry
3 tablespoons tinned	pepper

Slice chicken into matchstick-sized strips. Rub chicken, ham and abalone with salt and cornflour.

Bring 'broth' to boil in a saucepan. Add chicken, ham, abalone. Simmer gently for 3 minutes. Add sherry and adjust the seasonings. Stir and serve.

LAMB AND LEEK SOUP

PREPARATION TIME: 3–4 minutes. COOKING TIME: 8–9 minutes.

¼ lb lamb	1½ pints 'broth' (see pp.18–19)
½ teaspoon salt	1½ tablespoons soya sauce
2 teaspoons cornflour	1 tablespoon sherry
3 stalks young leeks	pepper

Cut lamb into very thin 1-inch × ½-inch slices. Rub with salt and cornflour. Cut leek into 1-inch pieces.

Bring ¾ pint water to boil in a saucepan. Add leeks and simmer for 3 minutes. Pour away half the water. Pour in the 'broth'. Bring to boil, add the lamb and simmer together for 5 minutes. Add soya sauce and sherry. Adjust the seasonings and serve.

GREEN AND WHITE SOUP

PREPARATION TIME: 2–3 minutes. COOKING TIME: 5–6 minutes.

1 tin green pea soup	water
1 cup 'broth' (see pp.18–19)	1 cup Fu-yung sauce (see
1 teaspoon salt	pp.20–21)
2 tablespoons cornflour,	½ cup milk
blended in 3 tablespoons	pepper

Heat pea soup in a saucepan. Add half the 'broth' and half the salt, and thicken with half the cornflour.

Heat remaining 'broth', Fu-yung sauce and milk in a second saucepan. Add remaining salt, and thicken with remaining cornflour.

When the contents of both saucepans are piping hot, adjust the seasonings, stir and pour the green soup into a wide open soup-bowl or tureen. Pour the white soup into the middle of the green soup. They can be poured and served in individual soup dishes in the same manner if so desired. The two contrasting colours and flavours make for an interesting presentation.

WHITE FISH AND GREEN PEA SOUP

PREPARATION TIME: 3–4 minutes. COOKING TIME: 3–4 minutes.

½ lb fillet of white fish (sole,
halibut, haddock, cod,
mullet, bream, bass, etc)
1 egg white
1 tablespoon cornflour
1 teaspoon salt

2 cans green pea soup
1 cup 'broth' (see pp.18–19)
2 teaspoons fresh lemon
juice
2 tablespoons sherry

Cut fish into 1½-inch × ½-inch slices. Beat egg white for half a
minute. Add cornflour and beat together into a batter. Rub the
pieces of fish with salt and coat them thoroughly in batter.

Heat pea soup in a saucepan. Add 'broth', stir and blend
well. When soup starts to boil drop in the pieces of fish one by
one. Allow the contents to simmer for 3 minutes. Sprinkle
soup with lemon juice and sherry and serve.

WHITE FISH AND SPRING GREEN SOUP

PREPARATION TIME: 5–6 minutes. COOKING TIME: 7–8 minutes.

½ lb fillet of white fish (sole,
halibut, haddock, cod,
bream, bass, etc)
1 egg white
1½ tablespoons cornflour
1½ teaspoons salt

½ lb heart of spring greens
1¾ pints 'broth' (see pp.18–19)
2 tablespoons chopped ham
1 teaspoon lemon juice
2 tablespoons sherry

Cut fish into 1½-inch × ½-inch slices. Beat egg white for half a
minute. Add cornflour and beat together into a batter. Rub
the fish pieces with ½ teaspoon salt and coat them thoroughly in
the batter. Chop greens into 1-inch × 1-inch pieces, discarding
coarser leaves.

Boil the spring greens in pint of water for five minutes. Pour away the water. Add the 'broth' and remaining salt. When the contents start to boil drop in the pieces of fish one by one. Allow the contents now to simmer for 3–4 minutes. Sprinkle with chopped ham, lemon juice and sherry. Adjust for seasonings and serve as soon as the soup reboils.

CREAM OF FISH SOUP WITH SHRIMPS

PREPARATION TIME: 6–7 minutes. COOKING TIME: 6–7 minutes.

¼ lb fillet of white fish
1 pint 'broth' (see pp.18–19)
2 teaspoons finely chopped lemon-rind shavings
1 cup Fu-yung sauce (see pp.20–21)
1 cup milk
1 teaspoon salt
¼ lb shrimps, peeled

1½ tablespoons cornflour, blended in 3 tablespoons water
1 teaspoon lemon juice
2 tablespoons sherry
2 tablespoons chopped ham
2 tablespoons chopped watercress

Boil fish in a little water for 5 minutes, drain, and mince into a paste. Heat 'broth' in a saucepan with chopped lemon peel for 2 minutes. Add Fu-yung sauce, milk and salt. When the contents start to boil add the minced fish and shrimps. Stir until contents are well blended. When it reboils, thicken with cornflour. Add lemon juice, sherry, half the chopped ham, half the chopped watercress. Stir and allow the contents to simmer for half a minute. Adjust for seasoning. Pour into a large soup bowl or tureen and serve sprinkled with the remaining chopped ham and watercress.

HOT AND SOUR SOUP

PREPARATION TIME: 4–5 minutes. COOKING TIME: 50 minutes.

2 oz (4–5 tablespoons) lean
pork, sliced into thin strips
4 tablespoons thinly sliced
mushrooms (preferably
dried – see p.1)
3 tablespoons bamboo
shoots, sliced into thin strips
(optional)
3 tablespoons diced ham, cut
into ¼-inch cubes
1½ pints 'broth' (see pp.18–19)
3 tablespoons shrimps

3 tablespoons diced fish, cut
into ¼-inch cubes
2 tablespoons soya sauce
2 tablespoons wine vinegar
½ teaspoon salt
¼ teaspoon freshly milled
black pepper
2½ teaspoons cornflour,
blended in 4 tablespoons
water
1 egg

Add pork, mushrooms, bamboo shoots and ham to 1 pint of
boiling water. Heat for 3 minutes. Skim for impurities and
continue to simmer for half an hour. Add 'broth', shrimps, fish,
and soya sauce, and continue to simmer for 10 minutes. Add
vinegar, salt and pepper; thicken with cornflour.

Beat the egg in a bowl for 10 seconds. Pour it in a thin
stream into the soup along the prongs of a fork. Allow the egg
a few seconds to set and harden. Stir and serve.

Extra Quick and Easy Soups

CHINESE CHICKEN NOODLE SOUP

Chinese chicken noodle soups are served on festive occasions
in China. Each guest is given a bowl as soon as he or she arrives,
much as guests are given a glass of sherry or a cocktail when
they arrive on such occasions in the west.

PREPARATION TIME: 2–3 minutes. COOKING TIME: 5–6 minutes.

1 small packet egg-noodles
(or vermicelli)
1¾ pints 'broth' (see pp. 18–19)
1 teaspoon salt
2 tablespoons soya sauce

2 tablespoons sherry
3–4 tablespoons finely sliced
cooked chicken
3–4 tablespoons finely sliced
cooked ham

Drop noodles in a pan of boiling water to simmer for 5 minutes.
Heat the 'broth' in a separate saucepan. Loosen the noodles,
drain and divide into 4–5 bowls. Sprinkle with salt, soya sauce
and sherry. Pour boiling 'broth' into each of the bowls. Garnish
the contents of each bowl with shredded chicken and ham.

GREEN JADE SOUP

PREPARATION TIME: 1 minute. COOKING TIME: 7–8 minutes.

1¾ pints 'broth' (see pp. 18–19)
1 packet (¼–½ lb) creamed or
minced frozen spinach
1 teaspoon salt
1 tablespoon soya sauce

1 tablespoon sherry
2 tablespoons cornflour,
blended in 3 tablespoons
water

Heat 'broth' in a saucepan. Add spinach, allowing it to melt
and dissolve slowly. When it has dissolved, stir the soup. Add
salt, soya sauce, sherry and cornflour to thicken. Stir and serve.

SHRIMPS AND GREEN PEAS IN WHITE SOUP

PREPARATION TIME: 1 minute. COOKING TIME: 3–4 minutes.

¾ pint 'broth' (see pp. 18–19)
¾ pint Fu-yung sauce (see
pp. 20–21)
1 cup milk
2 tablespoons cornflour,
blended in 4 tablespoons
water

1¼ teaspoons salt
4 tablespoons frozen green
peas
4 tablespoons fresh shrimps,
peeled
1 tablespoon sherry

Heat 'broth', Fu-yung sauce and milk in a saucepan until the contents begin to boil. Thicken with cornflour and add salt, peas, shrimps and sherry. Reboil, simmer for half a minute and serve.

VEGETABLE SOUP

PREPARATION TIME: 4–5 minutes. COOKING TIME: 5–6 minutes.

2 pints 'broth' (see pp.18–19)
½ teaspoon salt
pepper
1 tablespoon soya sauce
4–5 tablespoons bean sprouts (optional)
4–5 tablespoons chopped

spinach
1 tablespoon chopped chives
4–5 tablespoons sliced cucumber
4–5 tablespoons chopped watercress
2 tomatoes, cut into quarters

Heat 'broth' in saucepan. Add seasonings and all the vegetables. Heat to boiling and simmer for 3–4 minutes and serve.

EGG-FLOWER SOUP (SOUP OF THE GODS)

PREPARATION TIME: 2–3 minutes. COOKING TIME: 7–8 minutes.

2½ pints 'broth' (see pp.18–19)
½ teaspoon salt
pepper

1½ tablespoons soya sauce
1 tablespoon chopped chives
1 egg

Heat 'broth' and ¼ pint water in a saucepan. Add salt and pepper to taste. Divide soya sauce and chopped chives among 4 soup bowls. Beat the egg in a cup or bowl for 15 seconds, pour it slowly in a small stream along the prongs of a fork into the 'broth' in the saucepan. Allow the egg 10 seconds to set. Stir, then pour the soup into the 4 bowls.

Rice

Since rice and noodles are two of the basic foods of China we shall deal with them before we deal with the great varieties of meat, fish and other savoury dishes.

Portions: all the following recipes are meant to serve 4–6 people.

Rice

BOILED RICE

PREPARATION TIME: 1 minute. COOKING TIME: 17–18 minutes.

The cooking of very few dishes is as controversial as 'boiled rice'. Many methods have been advanced, including the use of a Japanese thermostatically-controlled rice-cooker. To the average Chinese cook all this appears unnecessary fuss, since the cooking of 'boiled rice' is so easy. The following method is one of the simplest.

½ lb long-grain rice   ½ pint boiling water
¾ pint water

After rinsing, washing and draining the rice under running water for 10 seconds, place in a saucepan and add ¾ pint of water. Bring contents to boil for 1 minute. Lower the heat to a minimum, allowing the rice to simmer gently for 6–7 minutes, when it should have absorbed all the water in the pan, and appear quite dry. Pour in ½ pint of boiling water. Replace the lid firmly. Allow the rice to simmer for a further 4–5 minutes. Turn the heat off altogether; now allow the rice to cook in its own heat for the next 6–7 minutes (do not open the lid during this time). The rice should then be ready to serve, although it will stay warm for up to ½ hour.

VEGETABLE FRIED RICE

PREPARATION TIME: 1–2 minutes. COOKING TIME: 5–7 minutes.

Fried rice is popular in the west, I think, partly because it is a self-contained dish which is simple and convenient to serve, and partly because in Chinese restaurants there is a great deal of bits and pieces of foods which can be conveniently cooked into the fried rice to advantage.

Vegetable Fried Rice is one of the simplest forms of fried rice, and it can be the basis from which other fancier forms can be prepared. Fried rice is generally made from cold cooked rice, but I have found that it can be equally well prepared from hot cooked rice, so long as it is dry and flaky, and not sticky and messy.

4 eggs
1 teaspoon salt
4 tablespoons green peas
1 small can button
mushrooms
1 tablespoon butter
2 tablespoons 'broth' (see pp.18–19)

1 tablespoon soya sauce
4 tablespoons vegetable oil
2 tablespoons chopped onion
½ lb (approximately 3 cups) cooked rice

Beat eggs in a bowl for 10 seconds. Add half the salt.

Heat the peas and mushrooms with butter, 'broth' and soya sauce in a small saucepan over moderate heat.

Heat oil in a large saucepan. When hot add onion and stir-fry for a minute. Pour in the beaten egg. Tilt the pan so that the egg will flow and cover the whole bottom of the pan. Lower the heat to very moderate and scramble the egg and onion. Add rice, sprinkle with remaining salt. Turn and scramble the rice thoroughly with the egg, oil and onion. Pour in the peas and mushrooms from the small saucepan. Continue to turn, stir and scramble until all the rice is very hot. Do the turning, stirring and scrambling lightly without 'messing up' the rice. It is important that fried rice should be served very hot. This is best achieved not by turning up the heat, but by cooking over moderate heat for an extra couple of mintues.

MEAT FRIED RICE
(CHICKEN, PORK, VEAL, BEEF OR LAMB)

PREPARATION TIME: 2 minutes. COOKING TIME: 7–9 minutes.

Almost any type of meat can be used for frying with rice. The way to do it is to follow the previous recipe of Vegetable Fried Rice and to use 4–5 tablespoons of meat diced into cubes of about $\frac{1}{4}$-inch square. Fry the meat in 1 tablespoon oil in the small saucepan for a short while (chicken and beef for half a minute, veal and lamb for $1\frac{1}{2}$ minutes, pork for 3 minutes) before adding mushrooms, peas and other ingredients. After the meat has been cooked separately with peas and mushrooms for 1 minute over high heat, add the mixture to the rice for a final period of stir-frying. It is important to fry these additional materials separately first before assembling together in the final frying with the rice, if one is to avoid producing a messed-up dish. The meat will provide additional texture to the dish, apart from flavour.

FRIED RICE WITH SEAFOOD

PREPARATION TIME: 2 minutes. COOKING TIME: 7–8 minutes.

The majority of seafood – such as shrimps, prawns, scallops, crab, abalone – can also be fried with rice. The way to produce such a fried rice dish is to cook the seafood in the same way as meat is cooked in the previous recipe, and then add it together with other ingredients into the Vegetable Fried Rice, for a final period of stir-frying. Seafood does not generally require more than ½–1 minute of frying before being added to the rice. It can, therefore, often be cooked in the small saucepan along with the peas and button mushrooms at the same time after the initial frying.

It should be remembered that the Chinese concept of Fried Rice is a dry dish. It is never slopping with gravy. It is best consumed along with a bowl of soup, which is taken in alternate spoonfuls with the rice.

Topped Rice

'Topped Rice' is getting to be a popular dish because of its convenience – it being a self-contained dish. It can be eaten from a large plate sitting down in the lounge or watching television. It also saves the cook or housewife from having to make a series of dishes in order to prepare and serve a proper Chinese sit-down communal dinner.

Almost any mixed stir-fried dish with gravy (especially those which have been shortly braised after frying) is suitable for 'topping' rice. But if a pure meat dish is used it will be useful to have a pure vegetable dish to complement it. For instance, if we were to use Red-cooked Beef (pp.78–9) or Red-cooked Pork (pp.56–8), then Plain Fried Spinach (see p.165) or Cauliflower in Fu-yung Sauce (see pp.20–21) would be good vegetable dishes to complement them. When warming up pure meat dishes, it is often the practice to add a small amount of soya sauce and sherry, which seem to have the effect of rapidly livening them up.

Although many meat and seafood dishes – such as Ribbons of Beef with Onion (see pp.72–3), Sweet and Sour Pork (see pp.64–5) and Diced Chicken with Green Peas (see p.90) – will all serve very well for 'topping' rice, a small selection of recipes for Topped Rice Dishes is provided below to give just a few examples.

Portions: In all the following three recipes the portions are calculated for two persons, and boiled rice is presumed ready at hand.

TOPPED RICE WITH SLICED SOYA STEAK AND BROCCOLI

PREPARATION TIME: 2–3 minutes. COOKING TIME: 9–10 minutes.

1 lb beef steak	6 tablespoons 'broth' (see
4 tablespoons gunpowder	pp.18–19)
sauce (see pp.19–20)	2 tablespoons vegetable oil
1 small head of broccoli	½ lb (approximately 3 cups)
(approximately ½ lb)	hot boiled rice

Cut steak into 1½-inch × ½-inch thin slices. Turn them in gunpowder sauce and leave to soak for a few minutes.

Discard any of the coarser parts of the broccoli. Chop it into approximately 1½-inch square pieces or break into individual branches. Parboil the broccoli for 4–5 minutes and drain. Then place it in a saucepan, add 'broth' and continue to cook over moderate heat for 3–4 minutes.

Heat oil in a frying-pan. Add the sliced steak and stir-fry quickly over high heat for 1¼ minutes, reserving any left-over marinade (gunpowder sauce). Divide hot boiled rice and spread out on two well-heated plates. Arrange the sliced steak on one side. Replace the frying-pan over the heat. Pour in the broccoli and liquid from the saucepan and the remaining marinade. Stir-fry over high heat for ¼ minute, divide and pour the vegetable and gravy over the rice on the other side. This should be eaten with a spoon and fork – served in this manner the food cannot be eaten with chopsticks, which require bowls.

TOPPED RICE WITH DICED CHICKEN, SHRIMPS AND GREEN PEAS

PREPARATION TIME: 1–2 minutes. COOKING TIME: 3–4 minutes.

1 breast of chicken
1½ tablespoons cornflour, blended in 3 tablespoons water
½ cup 'broth' (see pp.18–19)
1 small packet frozen green peas

1 small can button mushrooms
½ teaspoon salt
4 tablespoons Fu-yung sauce (see pp.20–21)
2 tablespoons sherry
½ lb (approximately 3 cups) hot boiled rice

Dice chicken into ¼-inch cubes. Add half the cornflour mixture and mix well.

Heat 'broth' in a saucepan. Add peas, and mushrooms. Bring to boil and simmer over moderate heat for 3 minutes. Turn heat high and add the cubed chicken and salt. Stir for 20 seconds and pour in remaining cornflour mixture, Fu-yung sauce and sherry. Stir for another 20 seconds.

Divide and spread the rice on to two well-heated serving plates. Ladle out the chicken, peas, mushrooms and gravy over the rice. Serve piping hot.

'TOPPED RICE' WITH SWEET AND SOUR PORK AND FU-YUNG CAULIFLOWER

PREPARATION TIME: 5–6 minutes. COOKING TIME: 7–8 minutes.

½ lb (approximately 3 cups) hot boiled rice

Sweet and Sour Pork (see pp.64–5)

Since the recipe for Sweet and Sour Pork is meant to serve 3–4 people, it is advisable to reduce the amount of pork from 1½ lb to 1 lb.

Divide and spread the rice on to two well-heated serving plates and cover with the pork and sauce.

If desired, this dish can be prepared with an additional vegetable of your choice, which should be cooked separately and added to the pork just before the final stir-frying.

Noodles

There are many types of noodle dishes in China. The best known of these in the west is, of course, Chow Mein, which simply means 'fried noodles'. There are also Gravy Noodles and Tossed Noodles.

Portions: all the following recipes are meant to serve 2–3 people. They are especially suitable for providing a western snack-type meal on their own, although they are also useful as a supplementary dish to serve with a proper multi-dish dinner.

Chow Mein (or Fried Noodles)

Chow Mein is different from Italian spaghettis, mainly in that the noodles are given a topping of meats and vegetables only after having been fried in oil and meat gravy. Otherwise they are very similar – some say that Italian pastas were originally brought over from China by Marco Polo in the thirteenth century – and egg-noodles, vermicelli or even spaghetti can all be used for the purpose. As a rule Chinese noodles and egg-noodles (or vermicelli) only require 6–8 minutes' boiling before they can be drained and made use of; spaghetti generally requires boiling for 15–16 minutes before it is sufficiently soft for use.

As with Fried Rice, almost any stir-fried meat and vegetable dishes can be used to top the Fried Noodles. The following few recipes should provide instances of how these noodle dishes are cooked and set out.

CHICKEN AND MUSHROOM CHOW MEIN WITH FRENCH BEANS

PREPARATION TIME: 3 minutes. PARBOILING: 6–7 minutes. COOKING TIME: 7–8 minutes.

½ lb noodles
3 large mushrooms
3 tablespoons vegetable oil
1 chopped onion
½ cup shredded french beans
¼ lb cooked chicken meat, sliced into double-

matchstick-sized strips
½ teaspoon salt
1 tablespoon soya sauce
1 tablespoon butter
2 tablespoons gunpowder sauce (see pp.19–20)
2 tablespoons sherry

Parboil noodles for 6–7 minutes. Drain, rinse under cold running water and put aside. Shred mushrooms and clean thoroughly under running water.

Heat 2 tablespoons oil in a large frying-pan. When hot add onion and french beans, and stir-fry for 1½ minutes. Add mushrooms and chicken. Sprinkle with salt, and ½ tablespoon soya sauce. Stir-fry gently for another 1½ minutes over moderate heat. Remove all the contents from the pan with perforated spoon and put aside.

Return the pan to the heat. Add the remaining oil, butter and gunpowder sauce. Heat and stir together over moderate heat for ½ minute, when the oil, butter and 'gravy' should become well mixed. Pour in the parboiled noodles, turn and stir-fry slowly in the pan for 1 minute. Adjust the heat to low, and continue to stir-fry slowly for another 2 minutes, when the noodles should be heated through. Divide the noodles into two serving plates. Return the frying-pan over the heat. Add sherry and remaining soya sauce. Return the chicken, mushroom and french beans into the pan for half a minute of stir-frying over high heat. Divide the contents and top the two platesful of noodles with them.

CHICKEN AND SHRIMP CHOW MEIN
WITH FRENCH BEANS

PREPARATION TIME: 2–3 minutes. PARBOILING: 6–7 minutes.
COOKING TIME: 7–8 minutes.

Follow the previous recipe substituting ¼ lb (½ cup) of shrimp meat for mushrooms.

BEEF AND ONION CHOW MEIN
WITH WATERCRESS

PREPARATION TIME: 2–3 minutes. PARBOILING: 6–7 minutes.
COOKING TIME: 6–7 minutes.

½ lb noodles	2 large onions, thinly sliced
⅔ lb beef steak	1 tablespoon butter
1½ teaspoons sugar	4 tablespoons gunpowder
2 tablespoons soya sauce	sauce (see pp.19–20)
pepper	3 tablespoons chopped
3 tablespoons vegetable oil	watercress

Parboil noodles for 6–7 minutes. Drain, rinse under running water and put aside. Cut beef into very thin strips, add sugar, soya sauce and pepper, and marinate for a few minutes.

Heat 2 tablespoons oil in a frying-pan. Add onion and stir-fry over high heat for 2 minutes. Add the marinaded beef and continue to stir-fry for 1 minute. Remove and put aside.

Add the remaining oil, butter and gunpowder sauce into the same pan. Place over high heat. Pour in the parboiled noodles. Turn and stir-fry slowly for 1 minute. Turn down the heat to low, and continue to stir-fry slowly for another 2 minutes.

Divide the noodles on to two well-heated serving plates or bowls. Return the frying-pan to the heat. Return the beef, onion, etc, into the pan. Stir-fry for ½ minute over high heat and top the two plates or bowls of noodles with the onion and beef and sprinkle with chopped watercress.

LAMB AND LEEK CHOW MEIN

PREPARATION TIME: 2–3 minutes. PARBOILING: 6–7 minutes. COOKING TIME: 6–7 minutes.

½ lb noodles
½ lb lamb (leg)
2 tablespoons soya sauce
1 teaspoon sugar
paprika powder
3 tablespoons vegetable oil
3–4 stalks young leeks, cut

into 1-inch segments
1 clove garlic, crushed
1 tablespoon butter
4 tablespoons gunpowder
sauce (see pp.19–20)
2 tablespoons sherry

Parboil noodles for 6–7 minutes. Drain, rinse under running water, and put aside.

Slice lamb into double-matchstick-sized strips. Add soya sauce, sugar and paprika, and marinate for a few minutes.

Heat 2 tablespoons oil in a frying-pan. Add leek and garlic to stir-fry together over high heat for 1½ minutes. Add the marinated lamb, and stir-fry together for another 1½ minutes. Remove and put aside.

Add the remaining oil, butter and gunpowder sauce to the frying-pan. Stir over moderate heat. Pour in the parboiled noodles. Turn and stir-fry slowly for 1 minute. Reduce the heat to low and continue to stir-fry slowly for 2 minutes. Divide the noodles on to two well-heated plates.

Add sherry to the frying-pan. Reheat the lamb and leek in it over high heat. Stir-fry for ½ minute. Divide the lamb mixture in two and top the two plates of noodles with it.

PORK AND BEAN-SPROUT CHOW MEIN

PREPARATION TIME: 2–3 minutes. PARBOILING: 6–7 minutes.
COOKING TIME: 7–8 minutes.

½ lb noodles
½ lb lean pork
1½ tablespoons soya sauce
1½ teaspoons sugar
pepper
3 tablespoons vegetable oil
1 tablespoon butter

4 tablespoons gunpowder
sauce (see pp.19–20)
½ lb (2 cups) bean-sprouts
¼ teaspoon salt
2 tablespoons sherry
4 tablespoons 'broth' (see
pp.18–19)

Parboil noodles for 6–7 minutes. Drain, rinse under running water, and put aside.

Shred pork. Add soya sauce, sugar and pepper and marinate for a few minutes.

Heat 2 tablespoons oil in a frying-pan. Add pork and stir-fry over high heat for 2 minutes. Lower heat to moderate, and continue to stir-fry for 1 minute. Remove and put aside.

Add butter and gunpowder sauce into the frying-pan over high heat. Pour in the parboiled noodles. Turn and stir-fry for 1 minute. Lower heat to very moderate, and continue to stir-fry slowly for 2 minutes. Divide the noodles on to two well-heated plates.

Add remaining oil to the frying-pan. Turn the heat high. Add the bean-sprouts. Sprinkle with salt and stir-fry for ½ minute. Add 'broth', continue to stir-fry for ½ minute. Add the pork and sherry and continue to stir-fry over high heat for 1 minute. Divide the pork mixture into two parts and top the noodles with it.

CHOW MEIN WITH SHREDDED DUCK MEAT AND CELERY

PREPARATION TIME: 2–3 minutes. PARBOILING: 6–7 minutes.
COOKING TIME: 6–7 minutes.

½ lb noodles	1 teaspoon chilli sauce
3 stalks celery	2 tablespoons sherry
3 tablespoons vegetable oil	1 tablespoon butter
1 teaspoon sugar	4 tablespoons gunpowder
1½ tablespoons soya sauce	sauce
¼ lb (approximately 1 cup)	1 tablespoon chopped
shredded roast duck meat	parsley

Prepare noodles as in preceding recipes.

Cut and shred celery into thin strips.

Heat 2 tablespoons oil in a frying-pan. Add celery and stir-fry over high heat for 1 minute. Add sugar and soya sauce and continue to stir-fry for ½ minute. Add duck meat, chilli sauce and 1 tablespoon sherry and stir-fry together for further ½ minute. Remove and put aside.

Add the remaining oil, butter and gunpowder sauce into the frying-pan, over high heat. Pour in the parboiled noodles. Turn and stir-fry for 1 minute. Reduce heat to low and continue to stir-fry slowly for a further 2 minutes. Divide the noodles on to two well-heated serving plates.

Add sherry and chopped parsley into the frying-pan over high heat. Return the duck and celery into the pan. Stir-fry for ½ minute. Divide the duck mixture into two parts and top the noodles with it.

Gravy Noodles

Gravy Noodles take longer to prepare than Chow Mein, as they must be served with large chunks of meat which have been cooked slowly. But if the meats are ready, as is often the case in a Chinese kitchen, Gravy Noodles can take a shorter time to prepare than Chow Mein. In the recipes which follow, we presume the meat is ready. Serve these dishes with chopsticks; eat by lifting the bowl to the mouth and resting the elbow on the table, as we do in China.

GRAVY NOODLES WITH RED-COOKED PORK AND SPINACH

PREPARATION TIME: 1–2 minutes. PARBOILING: 6–7 minutes.
COOKING TIME: 5–6 minutes.

½ lb noodles	2 tablespoons vegetable oil
½ lb red-cooked pork (see pp.56–8)	1 clove garlic, crushed
½ cup gunpowder sauce (see pp.19–20)	1 tablespoon chopped onion
1 cup 'broth' (see pp.18–19)	¼ lb (3 cups) chopped spinach
1½ tablespoons cornflour, blended in 3 tablespoons cold 'broth'	2 tablespoons sherry

Parboil noodles as in the previous recipes.

Heat pork in half the gunpowder sauce in a small saucepan. Pour the remainder of the sauce into another larger saucepan, heat and thicken it with the 'broth'-and-cornflour mixture, stirring steadily. When hot, add the parboiled noodles, and turn them in the thickened sauce. Heat over low heat for 3 minutes. Divide into two large bowls.

Heat oil in a frying-pan. When hot add garlic and onion. Stir-fry for ½ minute. Add spinach and sherry. Stir-fry over high heat for 2 minutes.

Meanwhile, ladle the pork and sauce into the two bowls of noodles and top with the hot spinach mixture.

GRAVY NOODLES WITH SPICED BEEF AND TOMATOES

PREPARATION TIME: 1–2 minutes. PARBOILING: 6–7 minutes.
COOKING TIME: 4–5 minutes.

½ lb noodles
½ lb red-cooked beef (see pp.78–9)
½ cup gunpowder sauce (see pp.19–20)
1 cup 'broth' (see pp.18–19)
1½ tablespoons cornflour,

blended with 3 tablespoons cold 'broth'
2 tablespoons sherry
3 tomatoes
2 teaspoons chopped chives
1 tablespoon vegetable oil

Parboil the noodles as in the previous recipes. Cut each tomato into four.

Heat beef in half the gunpowder sauce in a small saucepan. Pour the remaining sauce into a large saucepan, reserving 1 tablespoon of it. Add 'broth' and place over moderate heat; when hot add cornflour to thicken.

Add the parboiled noodles. Turn them in the thickened 'gravy' for 3 minutes over low heat. Divide into two bowls. Add sherry to the beef, turn up heat.

Divide the beef and pour it, together with its sauce, on top of the noodles in the two bowls. Fry the tomatoes and chives quickly in oil and 1 tablespoon gunpowder sauce. Add to the food in the bowls to decorate.

GRAVY NOODLES WITH CHICKEN AND OYSTERS

PREPARATION TIME: 3–4 minutes. PARBOILING: 6–7 minutes.
COOKING TIME: 7–8 minutes.

½ lb noodles
1 breast of chicken (see note on p.86)

1½ tablespoons vegetable oil
1 teaspoon finely chopped lemon-rind shavings

1 teaspoon salt
1 cup 'broth' (see pp.18–19)
½ cup oysters (1 doz shelled fresh oysters)
2 tablespoons sherry
1 tablespoon butter
1 small can button mushrooms

½ cup Fu-yung sauce (see pp.20–1)
1 tablespoon cornflour, blended in 2 tablespoons cold 'broth'
1 tablespoon chopped parsley
2 tablespoons chopped ham

Parboil noodles as in previous recipes. Dice chicken into ¼-inch cubes.

Heat oil in saucepan. When hot add chicken and chopped lemon rind. Stir-fry for ½ minute. Add salt, and half the 'broth'. When the mixture starts to boil pour in the oysters. Turn and set at moderate heat for 1½ minutes. Pour in the sherry. Heat gently for another minute.

Meanwhile, heat the remaining 'broth' in another saucepan, together with butter, mushrooms and Fu-yung sauce, adding cornflour to thicken. Adjust for seasonings. Pour in the noodles and turn them in the thickened sauce for 3 minutes over moderate heat. Divide the noodles into two bowls. Pour the chicken, oysters and mushrooms over each bowl of noodles. Sprinkle with chopped ham and parsley.

GRAVY NOODLES WITH CRAB-MEAT

PREPARATION TIME: 2–3 minutes. PARBOILING: 6–7 minutes.
COOKING TIME: 7–8 minutes.

½ lb noodles
2 stalks young leeks
2 tablespoons vegetable oil
2 tablespoons chopped onion
1 clove garlic, crushed
¼ lb (1 cup) crab-meat (fresh, cooked or canned)
½ teaspoon salt
1 cup 'broth' (see pp.18–19)

2 tablespoons sherry
½ cup gunpowder sauce (see pp.19–20)
1 tablespoon cornflour, blended in 2 tablespoons cold 'broth'
1 tablespoon chopped chives

Parboil noodles as in the previous recipes. Cut leeks into 1-inch segments.

Heat oil in a saucepan. Add onion, garlic, stir-fry over high heat for ½ minute. Add leek and continue to stir-fry for 1 minute. Add crab-meat and salt. Stir-fry together for 1 minute. Pour in 4 tablespoons 'broth' and sherry. Stir and heat for a further ½ minute.

Meanwhile, pour the remaining 'broth' and the gunpowder sauce into a large saucepan. Cook over moderate heat and thicken with cornflour mixture. Add the parboiled noodles. Turn them in the sauce over moderate heat for 2 minutes. Sprinkle noodles with chives, and add ¼ of the crab-meat and leek mixture. Mix and turn with the noodles. Divide the noodles into two large bowls. Top the contents of the two bowls with the remainder of the crab-meat and leek.

Topped-and-scrambled Noodles

This particular style of noodles is very similar to the Italian Spaghetti Bolognese or Milanese, where the prepared sauce is mixed into the noodles by the diners themselves – except that, with the Chinese noodles, the sauce used is slightly more piquant, and the crunchy, shredded vegetables always served with noodles provide a contrast of texture. This adds a new dimension to the dishes which are, in fact, pasta with shredded vegetable salad.

TOPPED-AND-SCRAMBLED NOODLES WITH PIQUANT MEAT SAUCE

PREPARATION TIME: 4–5 minutes. PARBOILING: 6–7 minutes. COOKING TIME: 4–5 minutes.

This dish has the quality of being meaty, crunchy, piquant and filling, all at the same time.

Q.E.C.C.—4

3½ tablespoons vegetable oil
1 clove garlic, chopped
1 tablespoon finely chopped onion
½ tablespoon chopped capers
¼ lb (1 cup) minced pork
2 tablespoons soya sauce (heavy type if available)

1½ teaspoons sugar
½ teaspoon chilli sauce
4 tablespoons 'broth' (see pp.18–19)
½ tablespoon cornflour, blended in 2 tablespoons cold 'broth'
½ lb noodles

For accompaniment:

1 small plateful bean-sprouts
1 saucerful shredded cucumber
½ saucerful spring onion (in 1-inch segments)
½ saucerful shredded celeriac

½ saucerful shredded radish
1 sauce-dish chutney
1 sauce-dish mixed sweet pickles
1 sauce-dish vinegar

Heat oil in a saucepan. Add garlic and onion, and stir-fry for ½ minute. Add capers and pork. Mix and stir-fry for 1½ minutes over high heat. Pour in the soya sauce, sugar, chilli sauce, and 'broth'. Stir and leave to cook for 1½ minutes after reducing heat to low. Add cornflour to thicken. Stir and cook for another minute.

Boil the noodles as in the previous recipes, divide them into two bowls while still very hot and ladle a suitable quantity of the prepared meat sauce over each bowl of noodles (quantity depends on taste).

The various shredded vegetables and bean-sprouts are placed on the table for individual diners to mix with the noodles and meat sauce. Additional quantities of chutney and pickles can also be added if desired. This type of noodle is a favourite dish of the peasantry in North China, who would use bean-paste rather than soya-bean sauce for preparing the meat sauce.

TOPPED-AND-SCRAMBLED NOODLES WITH BEEF-TOMATO SAUCE

PREPARATION TIME: 10–12 minutes. PARBOILING: 6–7 minutes. COOKING TIME: 5 minutes.

Follow previous recipe, substituting beef for pork. Add 3 tablespoons tomato purée, and use only 1 tablespoon soya sauce. All the attending shredded vegetables and bean-sprouts remain the same.

TOPPED-AND-SCRAMBLED NOODLES WITH SHREDDED DUCK AND MUSTARD SAUCE

PREPARATION TIME: 10–12 minutes. PARBOILING: 6–7 minutes. COOKING TIME: 5 minutes.

2–3 teaspoons mustard powder
2 teaspoons cornflour, blended in 2 tablespoons 'broth' (see pp.18–19)
6 tablespoons gunpowder sauce (see pp.19–20)

1 tablespoon butter
1½ tablespoons vegetable oil
1 tablespoon chopped chives
½ lb (approx 1½ cups) shredded roast duck meat
½ lb noodles

For accompaniment:

1 saucerful shredded cucumber
1 saucerful shredded radish
1 small bowlful bean-sprouts

1 sauce-dish mixed pickles
1 sauce-dish chutneys
1 sauce-dish vinegar

Boil noodles as in previous recipes.

Blend mustard with 1 tablespoon water. Mix with blended cornflour. Heat butter in small saucepan. When hot add the mustard mixture and stir over low heat until it thickens. Add oil and gunpowder sauce and stir thoroughly. Pour sauce into serving bowl.

Divide the parboiled noodles into two bowls while still very hot. Sprinkle immediately with chives and shredded duck-meat. Ladle a couple of tablespoonsful or more of the mustard sauce over the duck and parboiled noodles. Toss and scramble them together, and eat in conjunction with all the attendant shredded vegetables, pickles, chutneys.

TOPPED-AND-SCRAMBLED NOODLES WITH SHREDDED CHICKEN AND HAM WITH PARSLEY DRESSING

PREPARATION TIME: 10–12 minutes. PARBOILING: 6–7 minutes. COOKING TIME: 1–2 minutes.

½ lb noodles
1 tablespoon chopped chives
6 tablespoons 'broth' (see pp.18–19)
1½ tablespoons chopped parsley

½ teaspoon salt
2 tablespoons vegetable oil
¼ lb (1 cup) shredded roast chicken
4–6 tablespoons shredded cooked ham

Boil the noodles as in the previous recipes and divide into two bowls while still hot. Sprinkle immediately with chopped chives.

Heat 'broth' in a small saucepan. As soon as it boils add parsley and salt, and remove from heat. Pour in the oil, stir and beat for about ½ minute. Pour this 'dressing' into a saucebowl. Divide and arrange the shredded chicken and ham over the noodles. Ladle on the dressing.

This dish is served with the same attendant shredded raw vegetables and pickles, as in the previous recipe, and it can be eaten hot or cold.

TOPPED-AND-SCRAMBLED NOODLES WITH VEGETARIAN DRESSINGS

PREPARATION TIME: 4–5 minutes. PARBOILING: 6–7 minutes.
COOKING TIME: None.

½ lb noodles   1 tablespoon chopped chives

For Peanut Butter Dressing

3 tablespoons peanut butter   2 tablespoons sherry
2 tablespoons vegetable oil   1 teaspoon chilli sauce
2 tablespoons soya sauce

For Cucumber Dressing

¼ lb (1 cup) shredded   1½ tablespoons vinegar
cucumber, sliced into   1½ tablespoons soya sauce
double-matchstick-size   2 teaspoons sugar
strips   1 tablespoon sherry
1½ tablespoons vegetable oil

Mix and blend the ingredients of the 'dressings' separately
and place them in bowls.

Boil the noodles as in the previous recipes and divide into
2–3 separate bowls. Sprinkle immediately with chopped
chives.

Each diner helps himself to the 'dressings' and shredded
vegetables, etc, as in previous recipes.

Pork

Pork is the most widely used meat in China. It is cooked both on its own as well as in combination with other foods (mostly vegetables). When cooked on its own, it usually requires very little preparation, but necessitates fairly lengthy cooking. In other words, it is usually economical in preparation time, but uneconomical in cooking time. The reverse is true when pork is cooked in combination; for then the meat has to be reduced to a required size before it is cooked or stir-fried, together with vegetables or other materials (which may also have to be reduced to similar small sizes and shapes). In these cases preparation usually consumes more time than cooking. However, in each method there are things which can be shortened or simplified in favour of economy and clarity. We shall deal here with both styles of cooking.

Portions: see under individual sections and recipes.

Red-cooked Pork

Pork is 'red-cooked' when it is slowly cooked in ample gravy or sauce or soya sauce with one or two other ingredients; in our case we shall simply use gunpowder sauce (see pp.19–20), which is the standard combination of ingredients for this type of cooking. The general technique of 'red cooking' is to con-

duct the last stages of the cooking very slowly over very low
heat and in very little liquid (not more than $\frac{1}{4}$–$\frac{1}{3}$ the weight of
the meat) in order that the taste and juices of the meat will not
all be dispersed or diluted into the soup. As far as possible the
meat should be cooked in its own juices, with the basic flavours of the other ingredients penetrating into it. As this form
of cooking consumes very little *preparation time*, and since *cooking time* can be thermostatically controlled and requires very
little attention, it is a favourite form of Chinese cooking that
can easily be classified as 'quick and easy cooking'.

RED-COOKED PORK (BASIC RECIPE)

PREPARATION TIME: 1–2 minutes. COOKING TIME: 2 hours.

1 3–4 lb leg of pork with skin	sauce (see pp.19–20)
3 tablespoons soya sauce	2 tablespoons sherry
5 tablespoons gunpowder	2 teaspoons sugar

Bring 1$\frac{1}{2}$ pints water to boil in a large saucepan. Add pork to
boil in the water for 10 minutes. Pour away three-quarters of
the water, together with impurities. Add soya sauce and simmer for 20 minutes, turning the pork over once and reducing
the liquid to about half. Transfer the pork and gravy to a
casserole with lid. Pour 2 tablespoons gunpowder sauce over
the pork. Turn the pork over in the strengthened liquid a few
times. Place the casserole in a preheated oven at 375 degrees.
After half an hour, turn the pork over and add sherry, sugar,
and remaining gunpowder sauce. Reduce heat to 350 degrees.
Cook for one more hour at this reduced heat, turning the meat
over once in that time.
Portions: The following dish (and 3 variations) should be served
with at least two other dishes, one of which must be vegetable;
all to be eaten with rice. The amount here should be sufficient
for 4–8 persons, depending on the other dishes served. What is
uneaten should be regarded as precious, and be kept to be used
again for another meal, either warmed up or cold, or cooked

with vegetables into a new dish. This also applies to most other Chinese meat dishes where a large piece of meat is cooked whole.

RED-COOKED PORK WITH EGGS

PREPARATION TIME: 3–4 minutes. COOKING TIME: 2 hours.

Repeat the previous recipe. Simmer 4–6 hard-boiled eggs (shelled) in ½ pint soya sauce for ten minutes and add to the red-cooked pork gravy during the last half-hour of cooking.

RED-COOKED PORK WITH SPINACH

PREPARATION TIME: 3–4 minutes. COOKING TIME: 2 hours.

Follow the Basic Recipe above. Quick-fry ½ lb spinach (after cleaning and removing coarser bits) in 3 tablespoons vegetable oil and ½ teaspoon salt for 2 minutes over high heat, and insert it under the pork in the casserole during the last 15 minutes' cooking, adding 1 additional tablespoon each of sherry and gunpowder sauce.

RED-COOKED PORK WITH CHESTNUTS

PREPARATION TIME: 3–4 minutes. COOKING TIME: 2 hours.

Follow the Basic Recipe above. Boil 1 lb chestnut-meat for 30 minutes (simultaneously as the pork is cooked), drain and add to the pork gravy during the last 30 minutes' cooking. An additional 3 tablespoons of gunpowder sauce and 2 tablespoons sherry should be added with the chestnuts.

Chopped Red-cooked Pork

The foregoing recipes require the pork to be cooked in a whole piece. However, to save time in cooking, as well as to facilitate easier mixing with other materials, pork is frequently chopped into smaller pieces before cooking. In the following recipes it is either cut into 1½-inch square pieces, or 2-inch × 1-inch oblong pieces, preferably with skin attached to each piece. In China we regard pork skin, when thoroughly cooked, as meat-jelly – excellent for eating with rice.

Portions: the 3 following dishes are meant for 4–6 people, to be eaten with rice and a couple of other dishes, one of which should be a vegetable.

CHOPPED RED-COOKED PORK WITH CARROTS

PREPARATION TIME: 3–4 minutes. COOKING TIME: 1½ hours.

2 lb pork (leg or shoulder)
3 tablespoons soya sauce
1 lb carrots
3 tablespoons gunpowder sauce (see pp. 19–20)
2 tablespoons sherry

Cut pork into 2-inch × 1-inch pieces, place in heavy saucepan, add soya sauce and bring to boil in half-pint water. Simmer for half an hour. Clean and cut carrots into 1-inch length triangular wedge-shaped pieces. Add carrots, gunpowder sauce and sherry to pan. Simmer over very low fire for a further 1 hour, turning the materials over a couple of times in the process.

CHOPPED RED-COOKED PORK WITH CHESTNUTS

PREPARATION TIME: 3–4 minutes. COOKING TIME: 1½ hours.

Follow the previous recipe, substituting 1 lb chestnut-meat for carrots. Boil the chestnut-meat for 20 minutes and drain before adding to the pork for 1 hour's simmer together.

CHOPPED RED-COOKED PORK WITH POTATOES

PREPARATION TIME: 4–5 minutes. COOKING TIME: 1½ hours.

Repeat the above recipe for Chopped Red-cooked Pork with Carrots, using 2 lb potatoes instead of carrots. Peel and parboil them for 3 minutes, and add them to the pork during the last half-hour of cooking, along with ½ cup of 'broth' (see pp.18–19) and 2 extra tablespoons of gunpowder sauce (see pp.19–20).

Unlike the majority of Chinese dishes, this should be eaten without rice, accompanied only by one vegetable dish.

RED-COOKED SPARE-RIBS

PREPARATION TIME: 4–5 minutes. COOKING TIME: 70 minutes.

2–2½ lb spare ribs
1 large onion
pepper or paprika
2 tablespoons sherry
3 tablespoons soya sauce

1 cup 'broth' (see pp.18–19)
2½ tablespoons gunpowder
sauce (see pp.19–20)
2 tablespoons vegetable oil

Boil spare-ribs in a panful of water for 10 minutes. Drain. Cut into individual ribs. Chop onion and add it to the ribs in a saucepan. Sprinkle with pepper (or paprika), sherry and soya sauce; add the 'broth'. Simmer gently under cover for ¾ hour, turning the ribs over 3 times, until they are nearly dry. Brush or rub the ribs with gunpowder sauce and oil, and place in a roasting-pan in a preheated oven at 400 degrees for 15 minutes. Serve; to be eaten with fingers.

Portions: sufficient for 3–4 people; to be eaten on its own as a starter.

White-cooked Pork

Pork is said to be 'white-cooked' when it is boiled, simmered, or steamed plain, without the use of soya sauce. When cooked in such a manner it is invariably eaten dipped in a number of sauces, which are provided in small sauce-dishes placed on the dining-table.

Portions: the following recipes are meant for 3–4 persons if served as a main course, or for 7–9 if served with a few other dishes. If there is any left over it can be re-used cold or reheated.

WHITE-COOKED PORK (IN WHOLE PIECE)

PREPARATION TIME: 1 minute. COOKING TIME: 1¼ hours.

3 lb pork (leg or shoulder)   1 tablespoon finely chopped
2 teaspoons salt   lemon rind

Place pork in 4 pints of water in a saucepan. Bring to boil and add salt and add lemon rind. Simmer under cover for 1¼ hours. Drain (reserving stock for other uses). When cold, cut pork into 2-inch × 1-inch size thin slices to be served in conjunction with the following dips:

(a) 3 tablespoons soya sauce mixed with 2 teaspoons chilli sauce;
(b) 3 tablespoons soya sauce mixed with 2 tablespoons vinegar;
(c) 3 tablespoons soya sauce mixed with 3 teaspoons mustard;
(d) 2 tablespoons soya sauce mixed with 2 tablespoons tomato ketchup and 1 teaspoon chilli sauce.

CHOPPED WHITE-COOKED PORK WITH HAM

PREPARATION TIME: 2–3 minutes. COOKING TIME: 1¼ hours.

2 lb pork (leg or shoulder)	2 teaspoons sugar
1 lb belly of pork (with skin)	1 teaspoon salt
1 lb bacon or ham	4 tablespoons sherry

Boil both types of pork and bacon in ample water for 15 minutes. Drain and pour away water. Chop pork and bacon into 1½-inch pieces. Place the meats, alternately interlaced, in a heavy saucepan. Add ½ pint water, sugar, salt and sherry. Simmer under cover over low heat for 1 hour. Serve in a bowl or deep-sided dish.

CHOPPED WHITE-COOKED PORK WITH ABALONE AND CABBAGE (OR CELERY)

PREPARATION TIME: 3–4 minutes. COOKING TIME: 1¼ hours.

Follow the previous recipe, substituting 1 10-oz can of abalone for bacon (adding the abalone only during the last 10 minutes of cooking), and Chinese cabbage, savoy cabbage or celery (cut into 2-inch pieces and added during the last 30 minutes). Serve in a deep-sided dish, placing the meat and abalone on top of the cabbage.

Roast Pork

CHA SHAO ROAST PORK
(OR BARBECUED ROAST PORK)

PREPARATION TIME: 5–6 minutes. MARINATING TIME: overnight. COOKING TIME: 30 minutes.

3 lb fillet of pork
1 cup gunpowder sauce (see pp.19–20)

1 tablespoon honey
3 tablespoons sherry

Cut pork along the grain into pieces 2 inches wide, 1–1½ inches thick and 5–6 inches long. Marinate them in gunpowder sauce overnight, turning the pieces over a few times.

When ready, drain (reserve marinade). Place the strips of pork on a metal rack over the roasting-pan (filled with a little water to prevent drippings burning) and insert into an oven preheated to 400 degrees. Roast for 20 minutes. Stir honey and sherry into the remaining marinade. Turn the strips of pork in the marinade for a second dip. Turn them over in it a few times and place on rack to roast again in the oven for another 10 minutes at the same temperature.

Serve by slicing the pork across the strip against the grain into ¼-inch thick slices.

Portions: serves 6–8 people.

BRAISED-ROAST PORK CHOPS

PREPARATION TIME: 2–3 minutes. COOKING TIME: 35 minutes.

2–3 lb pork chops (in individual pieces)
8 tablespoons 'broth' (see pp.18–19)

4 tablespoons sherry
2 tablespoons soya sauce
2½ tablespoons gunpowder sauce (see pp.19–20)

Braise or simmer pork chops in 'broth', sherry and soya sauce for 25 minutes over moderate heat, turning the chops over every couple of minutes (until they are nearly dried). Pour the gunpowder sauce over the chops, brushing them with a pastry brush until they are evenly covered. Place on a roasting-pan in an oven, preheated to 400 degrees, for 10 minutes.

Portions: serves 5–6 people.

TWICE-COOKED PORK

PREPARATION TIME: 3–4 minutes. COOKING TIME: 37 minutes.

2 lb pork (leg or shoulder)
2 tablespoons vegetable oil
2 teaspoons chopped capers
1 clove garlic, chopped
2 teaspoons chilli sauce
4 teaspoons (¼ cup) chopped

young leeks
½ teaspoon salt
2 tablespoons sherry
1½ tablespoons soya sauce
1½ tablespoons gunpowder
sauce

Boil pork in water for 30 minutes. Slice into thin 2-inch × 1½-inch pieces. Heat oil in a large frying-pan. Add capers, garlic and chilli sauce; stir-fry for ½ minute. Add pork and stir-fry rapidly over high heat for 2½ minutes and remove. Add leeks and salt to stir-fry in the remaining oil for 1½ minutes. Replace the pork in the pan. Add sherry, soya sauce and gunpowder sauce. Stir-fry together, still over high heat, for 1½ minutes and serve.

Portions: serves 3–4 people.

SWEET AND SOUR PORK

PREPARATION TIME: 3–4 minutes. COOKING TIME: 5–6 minutes.

1½ lb lean pork
½ teaspoon salt
½ tablespoon cornflour
4 tablespoons vegetable oil

1 red or green pepper
1 cup sweet and sour sauce
(see p.21)

Dice pork into ¾-inch cubes. Sprinkle and rub with salt and cornflour.

Heat 3 tablespoons oil in a large frying-pan. When very hot add pork and stir-fry over high heat for 7 to 8 minutes. Remove pan from heat and put aside.

Heat 1 tablespoon oil in another frying pan. Slice the pepper into narrow 2-inch-long strips. Add them to the hot oil to

quick-fry for half a minute. Lower heat and pour in the sweet
and sour sauce. Turn the pepper over in the sauce until the
latter thickens. Pour in the pork from the other pan. Stir-fry
them together over high heat, stirring slowly for half a minute,
and serve.

Portions: serves 3–4 people.

Stir-fried Pork Dishes

The pork in the following recipes is either cut into thin slices,
or 'shredded' into matchstick-sized strips, or minced. Being
stir-fried, it usually takes only a short time to cook, but a somewhat longer time to prepare. In stir-fried dishes the size and
shape of the meat pieces depend largely upon the size and shape
of the other materials with which they will be cooked or served.
For instance, in cooking with bean-sprouts or ribbons of
onion, or in serving with noodles, the meat is invariably cut
into strips or shreds; on the other hand, when the meat is intended to be cooked with flat slices of sweet pepper, cucumber,
cabbage or mushrooms, the meat is generally cut into flat thin
slices.

Portions: all the following recipes are meant for 3–4 persons,
when eaten with rice, along with at least two other dishes. They
are sufficient for 7–8 persons, if the total number of dishes on
the table is increased by 2–3. They are also suitable as a topping
for noodles or rice (see Chow Mein [pp.42–7] and Topped
Rice [pp.38–41] to form a self-contained meal for 1–2 people).

STIR-FRIED PORK WITH BEAN-SPROUTS

PREPARATION TIME: 3–4 minutes. COOKING TIME: 6–7 minutes.

¾ lb lean pork
3 tablespoons vegetable oil
1 tablespoon soya sauce
½ teaspoon salt
pepper
1 clove garlic, crushed
2 stalks spring onion, in

1½-inch segments
2 tablespoons sherry
1 teaspoon sugar
1 lb bean-sprouts
3 tablespoons 'broth' (see pp.18–19)

Slice pork against the grain into matchstick-sized strips.

Heat 2 tablespoons oil in a large frying-pan. When hot add pork and stir-fry over high heat for 2 minutes, adding soya sauce during the second minute of stir-frying. Remove and keep hot.

Pour remaining oil into the pan. Add salt, pepper, garlic, spring onion, sherry and sugar. Stir-fry together over high heat for ½ minute. Add the bean-sprouts and continue to stir-fry over high heat for 1½ minutes. Add 'broth', replace the pork in the pan, stir-fry together for 2 minutes and serve.

STIR-FRIED SHREDDED PORK WITH SPRING ONIONS

PREPARATION TIME: 2–3 minutes. COOKING TIME: 5–6 minutes.

¾ lb lean pork
3 tablespoons vegetable oil
1 clove garlic, crushed
½ teaspoon salt
1½ tablespoons soya sauce
6 stalks spring onion, cut into 1½-inch segments

2 tablespoons sherry
1 teaspoon sugar
½ tablespoon cornflour, blended in 3 tablespoons cold 'broth' (see pp.18–19)
pepper

Slice pork into matchstick-sized strips (against the grain).

Heat oil in a large frying-pan. When hot add garlic, salt and pork, and stir-fry together over high heat for 2½ minutes. Add soya sauce and continue to stir-fry for 1 minute. Add spring onion, sherry, sugar, cornflour mixture and pepper. Stir-fry for a further 1½ minutes and serve.

STIR-FRIED SHREDDED PORK WITH CELERY

PREPARATION TIME: 2–3 minutes. COOKING TIME: 5–6 minutes.

Repeat the preceding recipe, substituting twice the quantity of celery for spring onion.

STIR-FRIED SHREDDED PORK WITH ASPARAGUS

PREPARATION TIME: 3–4 minutes. COOKING TIME: 8–9 minutes.

Follow the above recipe for Stir-fried Pork with Spring onions, using asparagus instead of spring onions. Remove the root-part of 4–6 stalks of asparagus, shred each stalk into thin strips and parboil for 3 minutes. Increase the final stir-frying by 1 minute with 2 additional tablespoons 'broth'.

STIR-FRIED SHREDDED PORK WITH PEAS AND MUSHROOMS

PREPARATION TIME: 3–4 minutes. COOKING TIME: 5–6 minutes.

¾ lb lean pork	1½ teaspoons sugar
1 small packet frozen green peas	1 tablespoon soya sauce
	2 tablespoons sherry
4–6 large mushrooms	1 teaspoon chilli sauce
2 tablespoons vegetable oil	½ tablespoon cornflour,
½ teaspoon salt	blended in 2 tablespoons
1 tablespoon butter	'broth' (see pp.18–19)

Slice pork into matchstick-sized strips (against the grain).
Thaw peas and slice mushrooms into strips similar to the pork.

Heat oil in a frying-pan. When hot, add the pork, sprinkle
with salt and stir-fry over high heat for 2 minutes. Remove and
keep warm. Add butter into the pan, along with peas and mushrooms. Stir-fry together for 1 minute. Add sugar, soya sauce,
sherry, chilli sauce, and return the pork to the pan. Stir-fry all
together for 1 minute. Add cornflour mixture. Heat for a
further ¾ minute. Turn over and scramble a few times and serve.

STIR-FRIED SLICED PORK WITH MUSHROOMS AND DRIED MUSHROOMS

PREPARATION TIME: 3–4 minutes. SOAKING TIME: 20 minutes (for
dried mushrooms). COOKING TIME: 5 minutes.

¾ lb lean pork
3 tablespoons soya sauce
4 dried mushrooms (optional
but preferable – see p.1)
8 medium-sized
mushrooms
2 tablespoons vegetable oil
1 tablespoon butter

1 teaspoon sugar
2 tablespoons sherry
¼ cup (mushroom) water (see
p.1)
½ tablespoon cornflour,
blended in 4 tablespoons
'broth' (see pp.18–19)

Cut pork with sharp knife into very thin 1½-inch × 1-inch slices
and marinate them in 1½ tablespoons soya sauce for a few minutes. (If using dried mushrooms soak them in ¼ cup hot water,
which should be retained.) Remove stems from mushrooms and
wash thoroughly.

Heat 2 tablespoons oil in a large frying-pan. Add pork, stir-
fry over high heat for 2 minutes and push to one side of the pan.
Add butter and stir-fry together both types of mushrooms for
1 minute. Add the remaining soya sauce, sugar and sherry and
scramble everything together for 1 minute. Pour in half the
(mushroom) water, and the cornflour mixture. Stir and scramble
together. Allow the contents to reboil and thicken, and serve.

STIR-FRIED SLICED PORK WITH CABBAGE

PREPARATION TIME: 3–4 minutes. COOKING TIME: 7–8 minutes.

¾ lb lean pork
½ lb cabbage (Chinese or savoy)
4 tablespoons vegetable oil
1 clove garlic, crushed
1½ teaspoons salt

1½ teaspoons sugar
2 tablespoons sherry
½ tablespoon cornflour, blended in 4 tablespoons 'broth' (see pp.18–19)

Cut pork into very thin 2-inch × 1½-inch slices. Cut cabbage into similar-sized pieces, discarding coarser parts.

Heat 2 tablespoons oil in a large frying-pan. Add pork, garlic and half the salt. Stir-fry over high heat for 2 minutes and push to one side of the pan. Pour remaining oil into the middle of the pan and add the cabbage. Stir-fry over high heat for 1½ minutes. Add sugar, remaining salt and sherry. Bring the pork in from the sides and stir-fry together for 2 minutes over moderate heat. Add the cornflour mixture. Turn and scramble together a few times. Allow the contents to heat for a further 2 minutes under cover over moderate heat.

Give them a final 10 seconds' stir-fry (adjust for seasonings, or add a few drops more of sherry) and serve.

STIR-FRIED SLICED PORK WITH CUCUMBER

PREPARATION TIME: 3–4 minutes. COOKING TIME: 7–8 minutes.

Repeat the preceding recipe, substituting sliced cucumber for cabbage. The last heating together can be reduced from 2 minutes to 1 minute before the final stir-fry.

Minced Pork Dishes

Portions: all the following recipes are meant to serve 3–4 people, when eaten with rice and at least 2 other dishes.

STEAMED MINCED PORK 'PUDDING' WITH CAULIFLOWER

PREPARATION TIME: 4–5 minutes. COOKING TIME: 1 hour.

1 egg	1 medium-sized cauliflower
1 lb minced pork	½ teaspoon salt
2 tablespoons cornflour	pepper
1½ tablespoons soya sauce	2 tablespoons sherry
2 teaspoons chopped pickles	

Beat egg and mix with minced pork, cornflour, soya sauce, and chopped pickles into a 'paste'. Break the cauliflower into individual branches. Pack the branches at the bottom of a large, deep, heat-proof basin. Sprinkle with salt, pepper and sherry. Pack minced-pork 'paste' in a thick layer over the cauliflower, sealing all the sides. Cover the top of basin with foil and place it in a large saucepan or boiler, standing in about 1½ inches of boiling water. Steam or double-boil the contents for 1 hour and serve in the original basin or heatproof dish. (Add more boiling water into saucepan or boiler when necessary.)

STUFFED SWEET PEPPERS

PREPARATION TIME: 3–4 minutes. COOKING TIME: 15–16 minutes.

4 large red or green peppers	1 teaspoon chopped capers
2 tablespoons vegetable oil	1 clove garlic, chopped
1 chilli pepper, chopped (or ¼ teaspoon chilli sauce)	2 teaspoons chopped chives or spring onion

¼ lb minced pork

1 tablespoon soya sauce

1½ teaspoons sugar

¾ tablespoon cornflour, blended in 3 tablespoons

'broth' (see pp.18–19)

1 tablespoon sherry

2 tablespoons chopped ham

1 tablespoon chopped parsley

Slice off ⅓ of the top of each pepper, and chop into a fine mince (discarding stem). Scrape out the soft insides of the peppers.

Heat oil in a frying-pan. Add chopped chilli pepper, capers, garlic, chives and chopped sweet pepper. Stir-fry together for ½ minute. Add minced pork and stir-fry together for 2 minutes. Add soya sauce, sugar, cornflour mixture, and sherry. Stir-fry together for 1½ minutes. Stuff the cooked minced meat mixture into the peppers and arrange them on a heatproof dish and place in an oven (preheated to 400 degrees) for 10 minutes. Sprinkle with chopped ham and parsley and serve.

MINCED PORKBALLS WITH CABBAGE (CHINESE OR SAVOY)

PREPARATION TIME: 3–4 minutes. COOKING TIME: 45–50 minutes.

¾ lb minced pork

1 tablespoon finely chopped chives

2½ tablespoons cornflour

½ beaten egg

1 tablespoon soya sauce

1 lb cabbage

½ pint 'broth' (see pp.18–19)

2 tablespoons sherry

1 teaspoon salt

pepper

Mix pork, chives, cornflour, egg and soya sauce into a paste and form paste into 6–8 balls.

Chop cabbage into 2-inch-long pieces. Place at the bottom of a casserole. Pour in 'broth' and sherry; sprinkle with salt and pepper. Arrange the porkballs on top of the cabbage. Close the lid of the casserole and insert into an oven, pre-heated at 375 degrees, for 45–50 minutes. Serve by bringing the casserole to the table.

Beef

As there are practically no dairy farms in China – cows and oxen being regarded as beasts of burden – beef is not as widely used as pork. However, in the areas bordering on Manchuria, Inner Mongolia and Sinkiang, which are mostly grasslands, cattle-raising is one of the principal activities. Beef is, therefore, a commoner dish in the North and frontier regions than in the South. But this does not mean that beef dishes are not obtainable everywhere in China. There are actually quite a number of them. In fact, practically all pork dishes can be made with beef, except that the long-cooked dishes require longer cooking than pork, and the quick-cooked dishes require shorter cooking than pork. Let us start with a few quick-cooked dishes.

Portions: all the following recipes are meant for 3–4 people when served with rice, soup and 2 other dishes.

QUICK-FRIED RIBBONS OF BEEF WITH ONIONS

PREPARATION TIME: 3–4 minutes. MARINATING TIME: 10–30 minutes. COOKING TIME: 3–3½ minutes.

1½ lb beef steak (fillet or rump)
2 large onions

2½ tablespoons soya sauce
2 tablespoons sherry
2 teaspoons sugar

¼ teaspoon chilli sauce
½ tablespoon shredded root
ginger (or finely chopped
lemon-rind shavings)

½ tablespoon cornflour,
blended in 2 tablespoons
chicken stock
4 tablespoons vegetable oil

Cut beef into strips or ribbons 1½ inches × ½ inch. Cut onions into very thin slices. Mix all the seasonings and cornflour mixture in a large bowl. Add the shredded beef and work the sauce into the beef with fingers. Leave to stand for 10–30 minutes.

Heat the oil in a large frying-pan. When very hot add the onions and stir-fry quickly over high heat for 2 minutes. Push them to one side of the pan. Pour the meat mixture into the centre of the pan. Stir-fry, spread it out, and scramble for 1½ minutes over high heat. Bring in the onions from the sides of the pan to mix and scramble together with the beef for ¾ minute. Turn out on to a well-heated serving dish and serve immediately.

QUICK-FRIED RIBBONS OF BEEF WITH BEAN-SPROUTS

PREPARATION TIME: 2–3 minutes. COOKING TIME: 2½ minutes.

¾–1 lb beef steak
2 teaspoons cornflour
1 teaspoon sugar
pepper
1½ tablespoons soya sauce
4 tablespoons vegetable oil

1 lb bean-sprouts
1 teaspoon salt
2 tablespoons 'broth' (see
pp.18–19)
2 tablespoons sherry

Cut beef into thin strips or ribbons. Sprinkle with cornflour, sugar, pepper and soya sauce, and mix everything well together.

Heat 2 tablespoons oil in a large saucepan. When very hot add the bean-sprouts and salt, and stir-fry at high heat for 2 minutes. Remove and keep warm.

Pour remaining oil into the pan. Add beef and stir-fry at high heat for ½ minute. Return the bean-sprouts to the pan, add 'broth' and sherry and stir-fry together for a further minute. Serve to be eaten immediately.

QUICK-FRIED RIBBONS OF BEEF WITH YOUNG LEEKS

PREPARATION TIME: 3–4 minutes. COOKING TIME: 5 minutes.

Follow the preceding recipe, substituting ½ lb thinly sliced leeks for bean-sprouts. Stir-fry them 3 minutes longer over high heat in the initial frying.

QUICK-FRIED RIBBONS OF BEEF WITH GREEN PEAS

PREPARATION TIME: 2–3 minutes. COOKING TIME: 2–3 minutes.

1 small packet frozen green peas
¾ lb beef steak
2 teaspoons cornflour
2 teaspoons sugar
pepper
1½ tablespoons soya sauce
2 tablespoons vegetable oil
½ teaspoon salt
2 tablespoons 'broth' (see pp.18–19)
2 tablespoons sherry

Thaw peas. Cut beef into shreds or ribbons. Sprinkle with cornflour, sugar, pepper and soya sauce, and rub into the meat.

Heat oil in a large frying-pan. When hot add beef to stir-fry for ½ minute. Pour in the peas, and all the other ingredients. Continue to stir-fry together over high heat for 1½ minutes. Serve to be eaten piping hot.

QUICK-FRIED SLICED BEEF WITH MUSHROOMS

PREPARATION TIME: 3–4 minutes. SOAKING TIME: 30 minutes (for dried mushrooms). COOKING TIME: 2–3 minutes.

1 lb beef steak
½ tablespoon cornflour
1½ teaspoons sugar
pepper
2½ tablespoons soya sauce
3 tablespoons vegetable oil
6 large mushrooms (cleaned, de-stemmed and quartered)

4 dried mushrooms (optional but preferable – see p.1)
½ teaspoon salt
3 tablespoons sherry
3 teaspoons cornflour, blended in 4 tablespoons 'broth' (see pp.18–19)

Cut beef into very thin 1½-inch × ½-inch slices. Sprinkle with cornflour, sugar, pepper and soya sauce, and rub into the meat.

Heat oil in a large frying-pan. When hot add beef, and stir-fry over high heat for ¼ minute. Add the mushrooms to stir-fry together for 1 minute. Add all the seasonings and ingredients and continue to stir-fry over high heat for ½ minute. Serve to be eaten immediately.

QUICK-FRIED SLICED BEEF WITH SWEET PEPPERS

PREPARATION TIME: 2–3 minutes. COOKING TIME: 2½ minutes.

1 lb beef steak
½ tablespoon cornflour
2 teaspoons sugar
pepper
1½ tablespoons soya sauce
3 medium-sized red or green peppers

1 small chilli pepper (optional)
3 tablespoons vegetable oil
½ teaspoon salt
2 tablespoons 'broth' (see pp.18–19)
2 tablespoons sherry

Cut beef into very thin 1½-inch × 1-inch slices. Sprinkle with cornflour, sugar, pepper and soya sauce, and rub into the meat.

Cut sweet peppers into similar-sized pieces as beef.

Heat 2 tablespoons oil in a large frying-pan. Add peppers and chopped chilli pepper, and stir-fry together over high heat for 1 minute. Remove and keep warm.

Pour remaining oil into the pan, add the beef, and stir-fry over high heat for $\frac{1}{2}$ minute. Return the peppers to the pan. Stir-fry together for $\frac{1}{2}$ minute. Add all the seasonings and ingredients and continue to stir-fry for $\frac{1}{2}$ minute. Serve to be eaten immediately.

QUICK-FRIED SLICED BEEF WITH CELERY

PREPARATION TIME: 2–3 minutes. COOKING TIME: 3 minutes.

Repeat the preceding recipe, substituting $\frac{1}{2}$ lb ($1\frac{1}{2}$ cups) celery (well cleaned and cut into $1\frac{1}{2}$-inch × 1-inch segments) for sweet peppers, and stir-fry for $1\frac{1}{2}$ minutes instead of 1 minute in the initial frying.

QUICK-FRIED SLICED BEEF WITH CABBAGE

PREPARATION TIME: 2–3 minutes. COOKING TIME: 3 minutes.

Repeat the preceding recipe substituting Chinese or savoy cabbage (using only the tenderer parts) for celery. Serve piping hot.

QUICK-FRIED SLICED BEEF WITH KIDNEY

PREPARATION TIME: 4–5 minutes. MARINATING TIME: 5 minutes. COOKING TIME: 3 minutes.

1 lb beef steak	pepper
1 lb beef kidney (or pig's)	1 tablespoon cornflour

4 tablespoons gunpowder
sauce (see pp.19–20)
4 tablespoons vegetable oil
1 clove garlic, crushed
2 stalks spring onion,
cut into 1-inch segments

2 tablespoons sherry
1 teaspoon sugar
½ teaspoon salt
3 teaspoons cornflour,
blended in 3 tablespoons
'broth' (see pp.18–19)

Cut beef into very thin 1½-inch × 1-inch slices. Remove core
and membrane of kidney and cut into thin slices similar in size
to the beef. Sprinkle both with pepper, cornflour and gunpowder sauce; rub in and marinate for 5 minutes.

Heat 2 tablespoons oil in a frying-pan. Add garlic and kidney
and stir-fry for ¾ minute. Remove and put aside.

Pour the remaining oil into the pan. Add beef. Stir-fry over
high heat for ¾ minute. Add spring onion and return kidney
to the pan. Add sherry, cornflour mixture, sugar and salt. Continue to stir-fry together over high heat for 1½ minutes and
serve immediately.

QUICK-FRIED SLICED BEEF WITH OYSTERS

PREPARATION TIME: 5–6 minutes. MARINATING TIME: 5 minutes.
COOKING TIME: 2½–3 minutes.

Beef is often cooked with oyster sauce in China (especially in
Canton). As oyster sauce is no more readily available in the
West than fresh oysters, we might as well cook with oysters, as
we used to do in my province, Fukien.

1 lb beef steak
pepper
2 tablespoons gunpowder
sauce (see pp.19–20)
1 teaspoon chopped chives
2 teaspoons finely chopped
lemon rind
½ teaspoon salt

paprika
4 tablespoons sherry
12 oysters cleaned and
shelled (retain oyster water)
4 tablespoons vegetable oil
2 cloves garlic, crushed
3 stalks spring onion, cut into
1-inch segments

3 teaspoons cornflour,
blended in 3 tablespoons
'broth' (see pp.18–19)

2 teaspoons lemon juice
1 tablespoon chopped
parsley

Cut beef into 1½-inch × 1-inch thin slices. Sprinkle with pepper and gunpowder sauce and marinate for 5 minutes.

Sprinkle chives, chopped lemon rind, salt, paprika and 2 tablespoons sherry over oysters and marinate for 5 minutes.

Heat 2 tablespoons oil in a large frying-pan over moderate heat. Add garlic and pour in the oysters. Stir-fry gently (so that the oysters do not break) for ¾ minute. Remove and keep warm.

Add remaining oil into the pan and turn heat up to high. Add the marinated beef and spring onions. Stir-fry for ¾ minute. Return the oysters to the pan, along with cornflour mixture and remaining sherry. Stir-fry together over moderate heat gently for 1 minute. Sprinkle with lemon juice and chopped parsley. Serve to be eaten piping hot.

RED-COOKED BEEF

PREPARATION TIME: 5–6 minutes. COOKING TIME: 3 hours.

4–5 lb beef (shin or shank)
½ pint gunpowder sauce (see
pp.19–20)

Bouquet garni (1 small
sachet)
6 tablespoons sherry

Boil beef in a saucepanful of water for 5 minutes. Pour away water and transfer beef into a casserole. Pour in gunpowder sauce and turn the beef around in the sauce a few times. Add bouquet garni and sherry. Close the lid of the casserole firmly and place in an oven, preheated to 375 degrees, for ½ hour. Reduce heat to 300 degrees for approximately 2½ hours, turning the beef over every half-hour. Slice and serve with its own gravy. This beef is equally good served cold.

Portions: this recipe is intended to provide more than one meal for 2–3 people – unless there are 7–8 diners, it should be kept for later uses!

CHOPPED RED-COOKED BEEF WITH CARROTS (OR TURNIPS)

PREPARATION TIME: 2–3 minutes. COOKING TIME: 2 hours.

2–3 lb stewing beef
1 cup gunpowder sauce (see pp. 19–20)
1 lb (2 cups) carrots (cleaned and cut in ½-inch × 1-inch wedge-shaped pieces)
4 tablespoons sherry

Cut beef into oblong pieces, 2 inches × 1 inch × 1 inch. Boil in a panful of water for 10 minutes. Pour away water and transfer beef to a casserole. Add half the gunpowder sauce and turn the beef around in it a few times. Place the casserole in a preheated oven at 350 degrees for ¾ hour. Add the carrots, sherry and remaining gunpowder sauce to the beef, stir gently, and return to the oven. Cook at the same temperature for 15 minutes. Then reduce heat to 325 degrees and cook for another 50 minutes; serve in the casserole.

Lamb

Like beef, lamb is another favourite food in North China and the frontier territories. Lamb or mutton is considered even stronger-flavoured than beef, and is usually cooked with strong-flavoured vegetables and ingredients such as leeks, onions, spring onions, garlic, ginger, various herbs, wine sediment paste, and plenty of wine.

Portions: once again the portions of the following recipes are calculated for 3–4 people, to be eaten with rice, soup and two other dishes unless otherwise stated.

QUICK-FRIED SLICED LAMB WITH SPRING ONIONS

PREPARATION TIME: 2–3 minutes. COOKING TIME: 2 minutes.

1½ lb lamb (leg)
½ tablespoon cornflour
2 tablespoons soya sauce
½ teaspoon chilli sauce
2 tablespoons sherry

6 stalks spring onion, cut into 1½-inch segments
3 tablespoons vegetable oil
1 clove garlic, crushed

Slice lamb into thin 2-inch × 1-inch strips. Sprinkle with corn-flour, soya sauce, chilli sauce and sherry. Work the ingredients into the meat with your fingers.

Heat oil in a large frying-pan. When hot add lamb and garlic, and stir-fry over high heat for 2 minutes. Add spring onions, and stir-fry together for another 1 minute. Serve on well-heated dish; to be eaten immediately.

QUICK-FRIED SLICED LAMB WITH YOUNG LEEKS

PREPARATION TIME: 2–3 minutes. COOKING TIME: 2–3 minutes.

Follow the preceding recipe, substituting ½ lb (1 cup) young leeks (chopped into 1½-inch segments) for onion. The leeks should be added to the lamb after the meat has been stir-fried for one minute only.

Stir-fry lamb and leeks together for 3 minutes.

QUICK-FRIED SLICED LAMB WITH ONION

PREPARATION TIME: 2–3 minutes. COOKING TIME: 2–3 minutes.

Follow the above recipe for Quick-fried Sliced Lamb with Spring Onions, substituting two large onions (thinly sliced) for the spring onions. Stir-fry the onions together with lamb and garlic from the beginning with 1 additional tablespoon of oil, 1 tablespoon soya sauce, 1 teaspoon sugar and 2 tablespoons 'broth' (see pp.18–19).

QUICK-FRIED SHREDDED LAMB WITH
SHREDDED VEGETABLES

PREPARATION TIME: 3–4 minutes. COOKING TIME: 4–5 minutes.

1 lb lamb	4 tablespoons vegetable oil
2 teaspoons cornflour	¼ lb (1 cup) shredded celery
1½ tablespoons soya sauce	3 stalks spring onion, cut into
2 tablespoons sherry	1-inch segments

¼ lb (1 cup) bean-sprouts   2 tablespoons wine sediment
½ teaspoon salt   paste (optional)

Slice lamb into thin shredded strips. Sprinkle with cornflour.
Add soya sauce and sherry, and work in with fingers.

Heat 2 tablespoons oil in a large frying-pan. Add lamb and
stir-fry over high heat for 1½ minutes and put aside.

Pour remaining oil into the pan. Stir-fry celery and spring
onions together for 1 minute over high heat. Add the bean-
sprouts and salt. Stir-fry together for ½ minute. Push all the
vegetables to the sides of the pan. Add wine sediment paste into
the centre of the pan. Stir it in the oil for a few seconds (if no
oil is left, add 1 tablespoon). Return the shredded lamb to the
pan. Stir-fry the vegetables and meat together for 1 minute and
serve.

'TRIPLE-QUICK-FRIES'

PREPARATION TIME: 5–6 minutes. COOKING TIME: 5–6 minutes.

1 lb lamb (leg)   4 tablespoons vegetable oil
½ lb lamb kidney (after   2 cloves garlic, crushed
removing core, membrane,   2 tablespoons finely chopped
etc)   onion
½ lamb liver   1 teaspoon sugar
4 tablespoons soya sauce   2 tablespoons 'broth' (see
5 tablespoons sherry   pp.18–19)
1½ tablespoons cornflour

Cut lamb, kidney and liver into thin 2-inch × 1-inch slices. Add
1 tablespoon soya sauce and 1 tablespoon sherry to each type
of meat, separately. Sprinkle with cornflour and work in the
seasonings with fingers.

Stir-fry each type of meat separately, one after another, in 1
tablespoon oil (use 2 tablespoons for initial frying of lamb) for
1 minute and put aside. Finally, stir-fry the garlic and onion in
the remaining oil in the same frying-pan for ¼ minute, and re-

turn all the meats to the pan for a final stir-fry together, adding the remaining soya sauce, sherry, sugar and 'broth' for 2 minutes, over high heat.

'TRIPLE-QUICK-FRIES' WITH WINE SEDIMENT PASTE

PREPARATION TIME: 2–3 minutes. COOKING TIME: 5–6 minutes.

Follow the preceding recipe, substituting 2 tablespoons wine sediment paste (see pp.21–2) for the final 2 tablespoons sherry. The wine sediment paste should be added to the pan at the beginning of the final stir-fry, along with the garlic, onion and 1 additional tablespoon oil.

Portions: like roasts, the following 3 pure meat dishes are not necessarily meant for one meal, unless there are to be 9 diners. Any leftovers can be used for another meal (cold or reheated).

RED-COOKED LAMB

PREPARATION TIME: 2–3 minutes. COOKING TIME: 1¼ hours for lamb.

3–4 lb lamb
8 tablespoons gunpowder sauce (see pp.19–20)
6 tablespoons 'broth' (see pp.18–19)

1 teaspoon salt
2 cloves garlic, crushed
bouquet garni (1 sachet)

Chop lamb into 1½-inch cubes. Place in a heavy saucepan, and simmer in 2 pints of boiling water for 5 minutes. Pour away half the water and skim off the impurities. Add all the ingredients and seasoning. Simmer very gently for 1¾ hours, turning meat over now and then. Serve in a tureen or deep-sided dish.

STEWED LAMB IN WINE SEDIMENT PASTE

PREPARATION TIME: 2–3 minutes. COOKING TIME: 1¼ hours for lamb.

Follow the preceding recipe, using only 3 tablespoons of gunpowder sauce. Add 4 tablespoons wine sediment paste during the last half-hour of cooking.

STEWED LAMB IN WINE WITH TURNIPS

PREPARATION TIME: 3–4 minutes. COOKING TIME: 1¼ hours for Red-cooked Lamb.

Follow the above recipe for Red-cooked Lamb. Pour away all the water after the initial boiling. Add ½ pint white wine, together with all the other seasonings and ingredients and 1 lb turnips (2 cups), cut into 1½-inch axe-head wedge-shaped pieces. Simmer for 1¼ hours; adjust for seasonings and serve.

QUICK-DIPPED LAMB

PREPARATION TIME: 4–5 minutes. COOKING TIME = Eating time.

This is a kind of Chinese lamb fondue, which has to be cooked in a chafing-dish (charcoal heated, methylated-spirit heated or electric) on the dining-table. The dish or pan should be at least 3–4 inches deep and 10–12 inches in diameter, so that it will contain at least 2–3 pints of 'broth' kept at a rolling boil. (It should preferably be equipped with a lid – a large round casserole sitting on a fondue stand would serve the purpose.)

4 lb lamb
2 pints 'broth' (see pp.18–19)
3 stalks spring onion

½ lb (2 cups) cabbage or celery
1 packet egg-noodles

Slice lamb into paper-thin strips, approximately $2\frac{1}{2} \times 1\frac{1}{2}$ inches. Divide on to six plates and place on dining-table.

Cut spring onion into $1\frac{1}{2}$-inch segments, celery or cabbage into $1\frac{1}{2}$-inch-long pieces. Place cabbage on two plates and onion on one plate on the table.

Heat the 'broth' in the kitchen and bring it to the table in the chafing-dish (or fondue-dish) just off the boil, with some onion and cabbage added. The flame under the dish should be burning well.

Each diner will use his or her chopsticks to pick up a piece of lamb and dip it into the boiling 'broth' for not more than $1-1\frac{1}{2}$ minutes, retrieving it to dip into one of the following dips before eating:

Soya sauce and vinegar dip (2 tablespoons soya sauce mixed with 3 tablespoons vinegar)

Soya and sherry dip (2 tablespoons soya sauce and 3 tablespoons sherry)

Soya chilli dip (3 tablespoons soya sauce and 3 teaspoons chilli sauce)

Tomato ketchup

Mustard

When nearly all the lamb is consumed all the remaining cabbage is added into the now-enriched 'broth', along with noodles. The lid is placed on the chafing-dish to allow the vegetable and noodles to cook under cover for five minutes. Each diner then fills his own bowl with a ladleful of this excellent soup and noodles from the chafing-dish, so that the meal is finished off with soup – a delicious reversal of normal western practice.

Portions: for such a dish the minimum amount of lamb should be calculated at $\frac{1}{2}$ to 1 lb per person. For a party this main dish should be complemented by a couple of other quick-fried dishes to be eaten with a small amount of rice.

Chicken

Chicken, like pork, is considered a very versatile meat in China. It combines successfully with a great number of other food-materials to produce a vast number of dishes. Often, too, it is cooked and prepared with distinction as a dish on its own. Like the majority of Chinese food materials of this type, chicken is prepared and presented in the usual varieties of sizes and shapes: it is cooked whole, chopped into large pieces, cut into slices, diced into cubes, or shredded into ribbons. Each type of preparation has its own traditions and its traditional types of food materials with which it is combined.

As a rule, the smaller the sizes of the chicken pieces, the shorter the time they require to cook, but somewhat longer time is required to prepare them; on the other hand, chicken which is cooked whole, or in large pieces, usually takes very little time to prepare, but much longer to cook.

Chicken breasts: now that ready-packaged chicken portions are widely available, it may be more convenient to use 2 ready-packed 'breast portions' in place of the 1 (whole) breast of chicken called for in many of the following recipes.

Portions: all these recipes are meant to serve 3–4 people when accompanied by rice, soup and 2 other dishes.

DICED CHICKEN QUICK-FRIED IN SOYA SAUCE

PREPARATION TIME: 3–4 minutes. COOKING TIME: 2–3 minutes.

1 breast of chicken	1 clove garlic, crushed
3 teaspoons cornflour	2 teaspoons tomato purée
2 tablespoons soya sauce	1 teaspoon sugar
2 tablespoons vegetable oil	1 teaspoon vinegar
1 tablespoon finely chopped onion	1 tablespoon sherry

Dice chicken into ½-inch cubes. Place in a bowl. Sprinkle with cornflour and soya sauce, and work in with fingers.

Heat oil in a frying-pan. Stir-fry onion and garlic together over high heat for ½ minute. Add purée, sugar, vinegar and sherry. Continue to stir-fry for ¼ minute. Pour in the chicken spreading it around the pan. Stir-fry quickly for 1¼ minutes and serve at once; to be eaten piping hot.

DICED CHICKEN QUICK-FRIED IN SWEET AND SOUR SAUCE

PREPARATION TIME: 3–4 minutes. COOKING TIME: 2–3 minutes.

1 breast of chicken	1 tablespoon finely chopped onion
1 teaspoon salt	
½ tablespoon cornflour	1 clove garlic, crushed
3 tablespoons vegetable oil	6 tablespoons sweet and sour sauce (see p.21)

Dice chicken into ½-inch cubes. Rub with salt and cornflour. Heat 2 tablespoons oil in a frying-pan. When very hot add chicken and stir-fry quickly for ¾ minute. Remove and put aside. Add remaining oil, onion and garlic. Stir-fry together for ½ minute. Add the sweet and sour sauce. Continue to mix and fry together for 10–15 seconds. Return the chicken to the pan, stir-fry for ½ minute and serve.

DICED CHICKEN QUICK-FRIED IN 'HOT SAUCE'

PREPARATION TIME: 3–4 minutes. COOKING TIME: 2–3 minutes.

Follow the preceding recipe, substituting the following sauce-mixture for the sweet and sour sauce.

1 tablespoon soya sauce
½ teaspoon salt
1 tablespoon tomato purée
1½ teaspoons chilli sauce
1 tablespoon sherry

1 teaspoon sugar
½ tablespoon cornflour,
blended in 2 tablespoons
'broth' (see pp.18–19)

This is obviously a 'hot' dish, as is the following recipe.

DICED CHICKEN WITH SWEET PEPPER AND CHILLI PEPPER

PREPARATION TIME: 3–4 minutes. COOKING TIME: 4–5 minutes.

1 breast of chicken
2 red or green peppers
2 red chilli peppers
¼ teaspoon salt
2 teaspoons cornflour
3 tablespoons vegetable oil
1 clove garlic, crushed

1 tablespoon soya sauce
1 teaspoon sugar
2 teaspoons vinegar
2 tablespoons sherry
2 tablespoons 'broth' (see
pp.18–19)

Dice chicken and red or green peppers into ½-inch cubes. Chop chilli peppers into ¼-inch pieces; remove and discard pips. Rub chicken with salt and cornflour.

Heat 2 tablespoons oil in a frying-pan. When hot stir-fry the chicken in it for ½ minute. Remove and keep warm.

Pour remaining oil into the pan. Add garlic, both types of peppers, and stir-fry them over high heat for 1½ minutes. Add soya sauce, sugar, vinegar, sherry and 'broth'. Stir-fry for 5 seconds. Return the chicken to the pan and continue to stir-fry for ½ minute and serve.

DICED CHICKEN QUICK-FRIED WITH WALNUTS

PREPARATION TIME: 3–4 minutes. COOKING TIME: 3–4 minutes.

1 breast of chicken	4 tablespoons vegetable oil
¼ lb (1 cup) shelled walnuts	2 teaspoons soya sauce
1 teaspoon salt	1 teaspoon sugar
½ tablespoon cornflour	2 tablespoons sherry

Dice chicken and walnuts into ¼-inch × ½-inch cubes. Rub chicken with salt and cornflour.

Heat 2 tablespoons oil in a frying-pan. Tip in the walnuts and stir-fry over moderate heat for 2 minutes. Remove and keep warm.

Pour 1 tablespoon oil into the pan. Add the chicken and stir-fry over high heat for ½ minute. Add remaining oil, soya sauce, sugar and sherry. Return the walnuts to the pan, continue to stir-fry over high heat for ½ minute, and serve.

DICED CHICKEN QUICK-FRIED WITH CUCUMBER AND BUTTON MUSHROOMS

PREPARATION TIME: 3–4 minutes. COOKING TIME: 2–3 minutes.

1 breast of chicken	1 small can button
1 6-inch segment of a large	mushrooms
cucumber (scraped but not	1 tablespoon soya sauce
peeled)	1½ teaspoons sugar
½ teaspoon salt	2 tablespoons 'broth' (see
2 teaspoons cornflour	pp.18–19)
3 tablespoons vegetable	2 tablespoons sherry
oil	pepper

Dice chicken and cucumber into ½-inch cubes. Rub chicken with salt and cornflour.

Heat 2 tablespoons oil in the frying-pan. Add chicken and stir-fry over moderate heat for ½ minute. Remove and keep warm.

Add remaining oil into the pan. Tip in the cucumber and mushrooms. Stir-fry over high heat for ½ minute. Add all the ingredients and seasonings. Return chicken to the pan, continue to stir-fry together for 1 minute, and serve.

DICED CHICKEN QUICK-FRIED WITH GREEN PEAS

PREPARATION TIME: 2–3 minutes. COOKING TIME: 4–5 minutes.

1 breast of chicken	1 packet frozen green peas
½ teaspoon salt	2 tablespoons 'broth'
pepper	2 teaspoons soya sauce
2 teaspoons cornflour	1 teaspoon sugar
2 tablespoons oil	2 tablespoons sherry

Thaw peas. Dice chicken breast into ½-inch cubes. Sprinkle with salt, pepper and dust with cornflour. Heat oil in a frying-pan. When hot add chicken and stir-fry for ½ minute. Remove pan from heat, but keep hot.

Heat peas in a small saucepan with 'broth', soya sauce, sugar and sherry. Allow them to simmer together for 3 minutes.

Pour the peas and gravy into the frying-pan with the chicken. Turn the heat up to the maximum, stir-fry together for ½ minute and serve in a well-heated dish.

Sliced Chicken

Sliced chicken differs from diced chicken in that it is usually cooked with larger pieces of vegetables which may require a brief period of parboiling before stir-frying together.

SLICED CHICKEN QUICK-FRIED WITH CAULIFLOWER

PREPARATION TIME: 3–4 minutes. PARBOILING: 5 minutes.
COOKING TIME: 3–4 minutes.

1 breast of chicken	1 tablespoon soya sauce
1 teaspoon salt	4 tablespoons 'broth' (see
2 teaspoons cornflour	pp.18–19)
1 small cauliflower	2 tablespoons sherry
3 tablespoons vegetable oil	

Slice chicken with a sharp knife into very thin pieces approximately 1 inch × ¾ inch. Rub with half the salt and the cornflour. Break cauliflower into individual branches of about the same size as the chicken pieces. Parboil in water for 5 minutes and drain.

Heat 2 tablespoons oil in a frying-pan. When hot stir-fry chicken for ½ minute. Remove and keep warm. Add remaining oil and cauliflower. Stir-fry for ½ minute. Sprinkle with remaining salt and soya sauce. Add 'broth'. Turn the cauliflower over in the sauce a few times. Cover the frying-pan with a lid, and allow the contents to simmer over moderate heat for 2 minutes. Return the chicken to the pan. Add sherry, stir-fry over high heat for ½ minute and serve.

SLICED CHICKEN QUICK-FRIED WITH BROCCOLI

PREPARATION TIME: 3–4 minutes. PARBOILING: 5 minutes.
COOKING TIME: 3–4 minutes.

Follow the preceding recipe, substituting broccoli for cauliflower.

SLICED CHICKEN QUICK-FRIED WITH MUSHROOMS

PREPARATION TIME: 3–4 minutes. SOAKING TIME: 30 minutes (for dried mushrooms). COOKING TIME: 3–4 minutes.

1 breast of chicken	2 tablespoons butter
½ teaspoon salt	1 tablespoon soya sauce
2 teaspoons cornflour	2 tablespoons 'broth' (see
8 large mushrooms	pp. 18–19)
4 dried mushrooms	½ tablespoon cornflour,
(optional but preferable – see	blended with 3 tablespoons
p. 1)	(mushroom) water
2 tablespoons vegetable oil	2 tablespoons sherry

Slice chicken meat into very small pieces, approximately 1-inch square. Rub with salt and cornflour. De-stem and clean mushrooms thoroughly. (If using dried mushrooms, retain 3 tablespoons of the water in which they are soaked.)

Heat oil in a frying-pan. Add chicken and stir-fry over high heat for ½ minute. Remove and put aside.

Add butter and mushrooms. Stir-fry them together for 1 minute. Add soya sauce, 'broth', cornflour blended in (mushroom) water, and sherry. Stir-fry for ½ minute. Return chicken to the pan for a final stir-frying of ½ minute, and serve.

SLICED CHICKEN QUICK-FRIED WITH PIG'S LIVER

PREPARATION TIME: 4–5 minutes. MARINATING TIME: 15 minutes. COOKING TIME: 4–5 minutes.

1 breast of chicken	1 teaspoon sugar
¼ teaspoon salt	1 tablespoon soya sauce
1 tablespoon cornflour	½ tablespoon vinegar
½ lb pig's liver	4 tablespoons vegetable oil

1 clove garlic, chopped
2 stalks spring onion, cut
into 1-inch segments

1½ tablespoons gunpowder
sauce (see pp.19–20)
1½ tablespoons sherry

Slice chicken into thin pieces, approximately 1½ inches × ¼ inch. Rub with salt, and half the cornflour. Cut pig's liver into similar slices and rub with remaining cornflour; sprinkle with sugar, soya sauce and vinegar, rub this into the liver, and leave to marinate for ¼ hour.

Heat 2 tablespoons oil in a frying-pan. When hot add chicken and stir-fry for ½ minute. Remove and keep warm.

Add remaining oil into the pan. Add garlic and spring onion. Stir-fry for ¼ minute. Add the sliced liver. Continue to stir-fry over moderate heat for 2 minutes. Return the chicken to the pan. Pour in the gunpowder sauce and sherry. Stir-fry together over high heat for ¾ minute and serve.

Chopped Chicken

In China a chicken is often served chopped into 16 or 20 pieces. When prepared in such a manner the chicken is more often than not cooked on its own, with only flavouring ingredients. It is usually cooked by stir-frying, deep-frying, braising or red-cooking. Because it is not combined with or 'married' to other food-materials, there is a certain simplicity about this way of cooking chicken. However you will need a sharp chopper to cut up the chicken (through the bones), and you will also need to be adept at stripping the meat from the bones when eating it.

CHOPPED SALTED DEEP-FRIED CHICKEN

PREPARATION TIME: 4–5 minutes. SALTING: 30 minutes. COOK-ING TIME: 4–5 minutes.

In China deep-frying does not necessarily require a deep-fryer. It can be done in an ordinary frying-pan with a lid, or a large saucepan, except that you will have to turn the pieces of chicken or food over in $\frac{1}{4}$–$\frac{1}{2}$ pint of hot oil.

1 2-lb roasting chicken	1 tablespoon chopped onion
2$\frac{1}{2}$ teaspoons salt	2 tablespoons sherry
1 tablespoon lemon rind (finely chopped)	$\frac{1}{4}$ pint vegetable oil

For batter:

4 tablespoons flour	4 tablespoons milk or water
1 egg	

Chop the bird into approximately 20 regular pieces. Sprinkle with salt, lemon rind, onion and sherry. Rub the ingredients into the pieces of chicken with fingers. Leave to stand for $\frac{1}{2}$ hour.

Meanwhile, make batter by blending the listed ingredients together into a smooth mixture.

Heat oil in a large saucepan. Dip the chicken in the batter. Put a few pieces into the pan at a time (protect yourself with the lid from spluttering oil). When all the chicken has been added into the pan, and the spluttering has reduced, turn the pieces of chicken over with a pair of bamboo chopsticks or perforated spoon. Fry over high heat for 3$\frac{1}{2}$–4 minutes. Drain and serve to be eaten hot, dipped in tomato ketchup and salt-and-pepper mix (see p.22).

CHOPPED BRAISED-FRIED CHICKEN IN SOYA SAUCE

PREPARATION TIME: 4–5 minutes. COOKING TIME: 7–8 minutes.

1 2–3 lb roasting chicken	6 tablespoons 'broth' (see
3 tablespoons vegetable oil	pp.18–19)
2 tablespoons chopped onion	2 tablespoons soya sauce
1 clove garlic, chopped	4 tablespoons sherry

1½ tablespoons lard
2 stalks spring onion, cut
into 1-inch segments

3 tablespoons gunpowder
sauce (see pp.19–20)

Chop the bird into approximately 20 regular pieces with a sharp chopper. Heat oil in a large saucepan. Add chopped onion and garlic to stir-fry for 15 seconds. Add all the chicken. Stir-fry over high heat for 2 minutes. Pour in the 'broth', soya sauce, sherry. Turn the pieces of chicken over in the sauce a few times. Close the pan with a lid and allow the contents to heat under cover over moderate heat for 5 minutes. By this time, the liquid in the pan will be very much reduced. Turn the heat high, add lard, spring onion and gunpowder sauce. Stir-fry until the chicken is almost completely dried (as if it had been stir-fried only). Pour contents out immediately into a well-heated deep-sided dish and serve.

CHOPPED BRAISED-FRIED CHICKEN WITH
WINE SEDIMENT PASTE

PREPARATION TIME: 3–4 minutes. COOKING TIME: 5–6 minutes.

Repeat the previous recipe, substituting 4 tablespoons wine sediment paste (see pp.21–2) for gunpowder sauce, reducing the 'broth' used to half, and the braising from 5 minutes to 2 minutes. Lengthen the final stir-fry by 1 minute to enable the chicken to be turned a little longer and more thoroughly in the 'paste'. A highly aromatic dish.

CRACKLING DEEP-FRIED CHOPPED CHICKEN

PREPARATION TIME: 3–4 minutes. SALTING AND DRYING: 3 hours. COOKING TIME: 3½ minutes.

1 3–4 lb roasting chicken
2 teaspoons salt

1 tablespoon sugar (use malt
or barley sugar if available)

| 4 tablespoons soya sauce | 2 egg whites |
| oil for deep frying | 4 tablespoons cornflour |

Chop the bird into approximately 20 regular pieces. Rub thoroughly with salt. Place in a colander over a plate in an airy spot to dry for at least 3 hours. Heat sugar in soya sauce until it has melted. Allow the mixture to cool.

Heat oil in the deep-fryer. When very hot lower the pieces of chicken in a wire-basket to fry for 2 minutes, remove and drain thoroughly. Place the chicken in a basin and pour the sugar-soya sauce mixture over it. Turn the chicken over in the sauce a few times to ensure that every piece is well covered. Dip the chicken pieces in a mixture of 2 egg whites whisked for 2 minutes with 4 tablespoons cornflour. Return the chicken for a second period of deep-fry for 1½–2 minutes. Drain and serve. Chicken cooked in this manner should be eaten dipped in salt-and-pepper mix (see p.22), placed in small saucers on the dining-table.

CHOPPED SIMMERED CHICKEN IN
WHITE FU-YUNG SAUCE

PREPARATION TIME: 6–7 minutes. COOKING TIME: 45 minutes.

1 2–3 lb chicken	4 tablespoons sherry
¼ lb piece of ham	2 cups Fu-yung sauce (see
¾ lb broccoli	pp.20–21)
2 teaspoons salt	

Chop the bird into approximately 20 pieces. Cut ham and broccoli into similar-sized pieces. Sprinkle chicken with salt and sherry.

Line a casserole with broccoli, place the pieces of chicken over it, and the pieces of ham on top of the chicken. Sprinkle with sherry and cook for 40 minutes in an oven preheated to 400 degrees.

Meanwhile heat the Fu-yung sauce in a large saucepan. When

chicken is ready empty the contents of the casserole into the sauce in the saucepan. Turn the chicken, broccoli and ham over in the sauce for 5 minutes. Serve in a large bowl, tureen or deep-sided dish.

WHITE CUT CHICKEN

PREPARATION TIME: 1–2 minutes. COOKING TIME: 50 minutes.

1 2–3 lb young chicken	3 stalks spring onion, cut
1½ teaspoons salt	into 2-inch segments

Place chicken in a saucepan. Add 2 pints water, salt and the spring onion. Bring to boil and simmer for 20 minutes, turning the chicken over a couple of times. Remove pan from heat. Allow the chicken to cook and cool in remaining heat, under cover, for ½ hour.

Remove the chicken from the pan and place it in the refrigerator for 1 hour. When cold, chop it through the bone into 16 to 20 pieces. The pieces should then be reassembled or arranged neatly on a serving dish. They should be eaten dipped in good-grade soya sauce, soya sauce mixed with vinegar, or soya sauce mixed with sherry or with chilli sauce.

CHINESE ROAST CHICKEN

PREPARATION TIME: 10–12 minutes. COOKING TIME: 1 hour.

1 3-lb roasting chicken	3 tablespoons tangerine or
6 tablespoons gunpowder	orange peel
sauce (see pp. 19–20)	4 stalks spring onion, cut
3 teaspoons sugar	into 1-inch segments
2 tablespoons soya sauce	

Clean and dry chicken thoroughly. Stand it in the oven at 250 degrees for 5 minutes to dry further. Mix the gunpowder sauce with sugar and soya sauce into a marinade. Rub the chicken thoroughly with the marinade and let it stand for 1 hour, turning it occasionally and rubbing with the marinade again. Stuff the bird with orange peel and spring onion.

Place the chicken in the oven, preheated at 375 degrees, for 1 hour, turning the bird over occasionally.

Chop the bird into approximately 20 pieces and serve; or carve and serve in the normal western style.

LONG-SIMMERED CHICKEN WITH CABBAGE, MUSHROOMS AND HAM

PREPARATION TIME: 4–5 minutes. SOAKING TIME: 20 minutes (for dried mushrooms). COOKING TIME: 2 hours.

1 3–4 lb chicken	6 large mushrooms
2 teaspoons salt	4 dried mushrooms
1 lb cabbage	(optional but preferable – see
3 stalks spring onion, cut into	p.1)
2-inch segments	3 slices salami

Boil chicken in 3 pints of water for 10 minutes. Pour away ⅔ of the water. Transfer to a casserole, add salt. Place the casserole in an oven preheated at 350 degrees for ¾ hour, turning the chicken over once. Meanwhile cut cabbage into 2-inch pieces, prepare the spring onion, de-stem mushrooms and slice into narrow 2-inch strips. Cut salami into similar strips.

Insert the cabbage under the chicken in the casserole and strew the top of the chicken with spring onion, salami, mushrooms. Return the casserole into the oven to continue to cook at 350 degrees for another hour. Serve by bringing the casserole to the table. The chicken should be tender enough to take to pieces with a pair of chopsticks.

CURRIED CHICKEN

PREPARATION TIME: 4–5 minutes. COOKING TIME: 25 minutes.

1 2–3 lb young chicken
2½ teaspoons salt
4 tablespoons vegetable oil
¼ lb young leeks cut into
1-inch segments

1 small onion, chopped
1 clove garlic, crushed
2 tablespoons curry powder
½ cup 'broth' (see pp.18–19)
1 tablespoon soya sauce

Chop the bird into approximately 20 pieces. Rub with 1½ tea-spoons salt. Heat 3 tablespoons oil in a saucepan or sauté-pan and stir-fry chicken slowly over high heat for 5 minutes and remove.

Pour remaining oil into the pan and stir-fry the leek, onion and garlic over high heat for 1½ minutes. Add curry powder and remaining salt. Continue to stir-fry for 2 minutes. Pour in the 'broth' and soya sauce. Stir for 2–3 minutes. When boiling return the chicken to the pan. Turn the pieces of chicken in the sauce a few times. Close the lid of the pan firmly and leave contents to simmer gently for the next 20 minutes. Open the lid, turn the contents over once more. Serve in a deep-sided dish.

JELLIED CHICKEN

PREPARATION TIME: 4–5 minutes. COOKING TIME: 45 minutes.
REFRIGERATION: 3 hours.

1 2–3 lb young chicken
1 pint 'broth' (see pp.18–19)
1 teaspoon salt
4 tablespoons sherry
4 1-inch segments of a large
cucumber

1 sweet pepper
1½ tablespoons gelatine
powder
lettuce and parsley (for
garnish)

Boil chicken in 3–4 pints water for 35 minutes. Leave to cool in the pan. When cold drain and chop through bone into 16–20 pieces.

Heat 'broth' with salt and sherry. Add the cucumber (thoroughly cleaned) and pepper, both diced into 1-inch-square pieces. Simmer for 6–7 minutes. Remove the pepper and cucumber with a perforated spoon. Dissolve gelatine in a little broth. Gradually pour in the rest of the broth, stirring till well mixed together.

Meanwhile, arrange the chicken pieces, skin side down in a mould, and interleave with the red and green of the sweet pepper and cucumber. Pour the 'broth' over, and place the mould in a refrigerator for 3 hours or overnight to set.

When serving tip the gelatinized chicken and jelly out onto a serving plate, and set off by surrounding with a bank of lettuce, and garnishing the whole with a few sprigs of parsley.

PAPER-WRAPPED CHICKEN

PREPARATION TIME: 12 minutes. COOKING TIME: 5 minutes.

1 large sheet cellophane paper	1 tablespoon soya sauce
1 breast of chicken	1 tablespoon sherry
2 rashers bacon	1 teaspoon sugar
1 2-inch segment of a large cucumber	pepper
	oil for deep-drying
2 stalks spring onion	

Cut cellophane paper into 8-inch × 6-inch pieces. Cut chicken into 12 2–3-inch lengthwise strips. Cut bacon across lean and fat into 12 strips. Cut cucumber and spring onion vertically into similar strips.

Add soya sauce, sherry, sugar and pepper to the chicken. Allow the chicken to soak in the marinade for 10 minutes.

Place a piece of cellophane paper on a work surface in front of you, with the long side running from left to right. Place a piece of marinated chicken, horizontally, just below the centre of the paper. Add a strip of bacon, spring onion and cucumber. Roll up the pieces from the bottom (away from you) in a loose roll. When you are about 2 inches from the top flatten the roll, so that it looks like an envelope. Turn in the two sides and fold down the flap from the top, tucking it in under the two folded-in sides. Turn the 'envelope' over and place a dish on it to keep firm. Use all the materials and pack them into similar 'envelopes' with the eleven remaining pieces of cellophane paper.

When they are all ready, place 6 'envelopes' at a time in a wire-basket to deep-fry in very hot oil for $1\frac{1}{2}$ minutes. Remove from oil to rest for 2 minutes and then lower them into the hot oil again for another $1\frac{1}{2}$ minutes of frying. By that time the chicken should be well cooked.

The 'envelopes' should then be drained thoroughly and arranged on a well-heated serving dish, like a trayful of envelopes containing important messages. Diners pick them up with chopsticks and eat them on their own plates or bowls.

PAPER-WRAPPED CHICKEN WITH OYSTERS AND ABALONE

PREPARATION TIME: 15 minutes. COOKING TIME: 5 minutes.

Follow the preceding recipe adding 1 oyster, 1 strip of tinned abalone (the same size as bacon) and 1 sprig of parsley into each 'envelope'. Lengthen the initial frying by $\frac{1}{2}$ minute (to 2 minutes).

This is an excellent party dish.

RED-COOKED CHICKEN (WHOLE)

PREPARATION TIME: 1 minute. COOKING TIME: $1\frac{3}{4}$ hours.

1 3–4 lb chicken	1 cup gunpowder sauce (see pp.19–20)

Clean and place the chicken in a casserole. Pour 1 cup of water and the gunpowder sauce over the chicken. Place the casserole into an oven at 375 degrees (preheated) for ¾ hour. Turn the chicken over and reduce heat to 325 degrees; cook for another hour, turning the chicken a few times in the process.

This is a standby home-cooked dish, which requires very little work to prepare and cook.

DRUNKEN CHICKEN

PREPARATION TIME: 4–5 minutes. SALTING TIME: 2 days. COOKING TIME: 45 minutes. SOAKING TIME: 2–3 days.

1 2–3 lb chicken	2 tablespoons salt
6 onions, finely chopped	2 bottles of dry sherry

Mix onion with salt and rub chicken inside and out with this mixture. Let it stand for 15 minutes. Rub for a second time. Place chicken in an airy place to salt and dry for two days.

After two days rinse it quickly under running water, both inside and out. Pat dry with paper-towel. Place chicken in a casserole with 1 cup water. Put the casserole in an oven, preheated to 400 degrees, for 15 minutes. Reduce heat to 325 degrees for 30 minutes. Open the lid and allow the chicken to cool.

When cold, place the chicken in a jar. Pour in the two bottles of dry sherry. After 1 hour turn the chicken around and allow it to be immersed in the sherry for 2 days, turning it around every 12 hours.

When ready for use, chop chicken into 16 to 20 pieces. Serve as a starter.

Leftover Chicken

Leftover chicken meat is particularly suitable for dishes where shredded chicken is used, although the following recipes can also be made with fresh chicken. Shredded chicken is usually stir-fried with vegetables which are thread-like in shape, and is then combined with noodles or other foods of a similar shape.

SHREDDED CHICKEN QUICK-FRIED WITH BEAN-SPROUTS

PREPARATION TIME: 3–4 minutes. COOKING TIME: 2–3 minutes.

1½ cups cooked chicken meat
½ teaspoon salt
2 teaspoons cornflour
3 tablespoons vegetable oil
2 stalks spring onion, cut into 1-inch segments
½ lb (2 cups) bean-sprouts

1 tablespoon soya sauce
2 tablespoons 'broth' (see pp. 18–19)
1 tablespoon vinegar
2 tablespoons sherry
pepper

Shred chicken with sharp knife into thin ribbons. Rub with salt and cornflour.

Heat 2 tablespoons oil in a frying-pan. When hot, stir-fry chicken for ½ minute. Remove and keep warm.

Pour remaining oil into the pan with spring onions. Stir-fry for ¼ minute. Add bean-sprouts and stir-fry over high heat for ½ minute. Add all the seasonings and remaining ingredients. Stir-fry for another ½ minute. Finally, return the chicken to the pan for an assembly fry of another ¾ minute; serve.

SHREDDED CHICKEN WITH CELERY

PREPARATION TIME: 3–4 minutes. COOKING TIME: 2–3 minutes.

Follow the preceding recipe, using ½ lb (2 cups) celery (shredded to the same size as the ribbons of chicken) instead of bean-sprouts, and 1 teaspoon chilli sauce instead of vinegar.

SHREDDED CHICKEN QUICK-FRIED WITH SHREDDED MUSHROOMS AND BAMBOO SHOOTS

PREPARATION TIME: 3–4 minutes. SOAKING TIME: 30 minutes (for dried mushrooms). COOKING TIME: 3–4 minutes.

1½ cups cooked chicken meat
½ teaspoon salt
2 teaspoons cornflour
¼ lb (1 cup) shredded mushrooms (preferably dried – see p.1)
3 tablespoons vegetable oil
2 stalks spring onion, cut into 1-inch segments

1 cup shredded bamboo shoots
1 tablespoon soya sauce
2 tablespoons 'broth' (see pp.18–19)
3 tablespoons (mushroom) water
2 tablespoons sherry
pepper

Shred chicken into thin ribbons. Rub with salt and cornflour. (If using dried mushrooms, retain 3 tablespoons of the water in which they are soaked.)

Heat 2 tablespoons oil in frying-pan. Add chicken. Stir-fry for ½ minute. Remove and keep warm. Add remaining oil to pan with spring onion and bamboo shoots; stir-fry for ½ minute; add mushrooms, and stir-fry for ½ minute, then add remaining ingredients. Finally, add chicken for assembly frying of 1½ minutes.

SHREDDED CHICKEN WITH SWEET PEPPER AND CHILLI PEPPER RIBBONS

PREPARATION TIME: 3–4 minutes. COOKING TIME: 3–4 minutes.

For those who prefer their food 'hot' this is a good dish to prepare. Follow the recipe for Shredded Chicken Quick-fried with Bean-sprouts, substituting 2 large red or green peppers (thinly sliced) for bean-sprouts and one or two chilli peppers (shredded) for spring onion. Since this dish is extremely 'hot', one chilli pepper is usually sufficient for most people.

Duck

Duck is a very popular food in China, though it is not as common as chicken. One of the reasons for this is that the flavour of duck's meat is stronger and, therefore, cannot be combined with other foods as easily or widely as chicken. For instance, there are very few diced duck meat dishes among Chinese recipes. Duck is usually shredded, sliced, chopped, or cooked whole.

One of the best known of Chinese duck dishes is 'Peking Duck' which is a roast duck. This dish is by no means a 'quick and easy' dish to cook, but it can be simplified. The following is a simplified version.

Portions: all the following recipes are meant for 4–6 people, when served with rice and at least two other dishes.

PEKING DUCK

PREPARATION TIME: 2–3 minutes. DRYING TIME: Overnight.
COOKING TIME: 1 hour 10 minutes.

1 3–3½ lb duck

Dip a cleaned duck in a pan of boiling water for 2 seconds. Remove and dry thoroughly. Hang it up to dry in an airy place overnight. Place duck on a rack (with water-filled drip-pan underneath to catch the drips) in an oven pre-heated to 425 degrees. After the first 10 minutes reduce the heat to 375 degrees. Allow the duck to roast steadily for 1 hour without basting. The duck skin will then be crisp and the meat well cooked.

Eating:

One of the distinguishing things about Peking Duck is the way it is eaten. It is eaten wrapped in a pancake. In serving this dish you will have to prepare at least 1½ dozen or more very thin pancakes, as well as provide a couple of small dishes each of 2-inch segments of spring onions sliced in half or quartered, and strips of cucumber cut to similar size. The duck meat and crispy skin, sliced while still very hot, are wrapped in a pancake by the diner, together with a piece of spring onion and cucumber. The pancakes are eaten after brushing them with a liberal amount of plum sauce, or blackcurrant jam and soya jam mixed together. (If soya jam is not available, use some thickened soya sauce, prepared by reducing it to half by heating slowly and adding some sugar.) Peking Duck is in fact a pancake dish (except that the pancake, often called a doily, is a very dry version, made without eggs).

PANCAKES (OR DOILIES) FOR DUCK

2 cups flour	blended with 2 teaspoons
2 tablespoons sesame oil (or	peanut butter)
2 tablespoons peanut oil,	

Sift flour into a large basin and slowly add 1 cup boiling water. Work with a wooden spoon into a warm dough. Knead 5 minutes and let stand for 10 minutes. Make dough into a long roll about 1½–2 inches in diameter. Cut off approximately ½-inch-thick pieces. With the aid of a knife, pat and flatten the pieces on a well-floured board into round thin dough-cakes of about 3-inch diameter. Brush the top of two dough-cakes liberally with sesame oil. Place one piece of 'cake' on top of another, greased sides facing each other. Roll gently from centre out into 6-inch-diameter double pancake, rolling on both sides. Repeat with remaining dough.

Heat ungreased heavy frying-pan or griddle over medium heat. Place pancakes two at a time to heat for 3 to 3½ minutes on either side, or until some parts bubble and begin to turn brown. When slightly cooler pull each pancake apart into two (the greased sides should detach themselves quite easily). Fold each pancake across the centre with the greased side inside.

Stack the pancakes on a heatproof dish, and place them in a steamer to steam vigorously for 10 minutes, when they should be ready for use. If no steamer is available place the heatproof dish with pancakes in a colander and set the latter over a pan of vigorously boiling water for 12 to 13 minutes. These pancakes can be stored in a refrigerator for several days, but will require 6–7 minutes of steaming again before using.

AROMATIC AND CRISPY DUCK

This is another version of Chinese duck dish whereby the duck meat is eaten wrapped in pancakes.

PREPARATION TIME: 2–3 minutes. COOKING TIME: 45 minutes.

1 2–3 lb duck	3 tablespoons sugar
2 pints gunpowder sauce (see pp.19–20)	bouquet garni (3 sachets)
	oil for deep frying

Give the cleaned duck a 3-minute dip in a pan of boiling water, and then place it to simmer for 30 minutes in the gunpowder sauce, to which the sugar and bouquet garni have been added. Drain the duck thoroughly and heat the oil in the deep-fryer.

Lower the duck in a wire basket to deep-fry in the hot oil for 8 minutes.

When ready the duck is served and eaten in the same way as the Peking Duck.

PAN-ROAST RED-COOKED DUCK

PREPARATION TIME: 2–3 minutes. COOKING TIME: 1 hour 15 minutes.

1 3-lb duck	1 tablespoon chopped lemon
6 tablespoons vegetable oil	rind
3 stalks spring onion, cut into	4 tablespoons sherry
1-inch segments	1 cup gunpowder sauce (see
	pp.19–20)

Heat oil in a saucepan. Add cleaned duck to fry over high heat for 5 minutes, turning it over all the time. Drain away oil. Add onion, lemon rind, sherry and gunpowder sauce. Continue to turn the duck over in the simmering liquid for 10 minutes. Transfer the duck and sauce to a casserole and cook for 1 hour in an oven preheated to 375 degrees, turning the bird over occasionally and adding a small amount of liquid (a couple of spoonsful each of water, sherry and gunpowder sauce) if the pan gets too dry.

The duck can be served and eaten carved in the normal western way, or chopped through the bone into 16–20 pieces and reassembled on a dish and served in the Chinese way with two or three other dishes; or the meat can be used to prepare other duck dishes.

CHOPPED DRY-FRIED RED-COOKED DUCK

PREPARATION TIME: 5 minutes. COOKING TIME: 25–30 minutes.

1 2–3 lb duck	$\frac{1}{4}$ cup gunpowder sauce (see
4 tablespoons vegetable oil	pp.19–20)
1 clove garlic, chopped	1 drop red food-colouring
1 tablespoon chopped onion	(or cochineal)

For final stir-frying

2 tablespoons lard   2 tablespoons sherry
2 tablespoons gunpowder   2 stalks spring onion, cut into
sauce (see pp.19–20)   1-inch segments

Chop the cleaned duck through the bone into 16–20 pieces.
Heat oil in a large saucepan. Stir-fry duck, garlic and onion together for 5 minutes. Drain away fat. Pour in ½ cup water and
gunpowder sauce, and add food colouring. Heat under cover
for 10 minutes, turning the pieces of duck over a couple of times.
    Turn heat up to the maximum, turning the duck over occa-
sionally at first and rapidly as the sauce starts to dry. Just before
the liquid is about to dry add the lard and all the ingredients for
the 'final stir-frying'. Stir-fry until all liquid is dry. Arrange and
serve on a well-heated dish.

CHOPPED DRY-FRIED DUCK IN
WINE SEDIMENT PASTE

PREPARATION TIME: 5–6 minutes. COOKING TIME: 25–30 minutes.

Follow the preceding recipe, using 4–6 tablespoons wine
sediment paste (see pp.21–2) instead of gunpowder sauce in
the final stir-fry.

DRUNKEN DUCK

PREPARATION TIME: 5–6 minutes. SALTING: 2 days. COOKING
TIME: 50 minutes. SOAKING: 2–3 days.
Follow the instructions for Drunken Chicken (see p.102).
Add 3 tablespoons chopped lemon rind into the mixture for the
salting, and lengthen the time of the initial heating in the oven
to 20 minutes.

Excellent as a starter; or serve at cocktail parties skewered on toothpicks (after removing bones and cutting into smaller all-meat pieces).

CLEAR-SIMMERED ORANGE DUCK WITH ONION, PORK AND CABBAGE (OR CELERY)

PREPARATION TIME: 8–10 minutes. COOKING TIME: 2¼ hours.

1 4–4½ lb duck
2 medium-sized onions
1 large orange
2 slices root ginger (or 1 tablespoon finely chopped lemon rind shavings)

1 clove garlic, crushed
½ lb (1 cup) roast pork, both lean and fat (chopped into 1 inch × ½ inch pieces)
2½ teaspoons salt
½–1 lb cabbage or celery

Dip cleaned duck in boiling water for 3 minutes and drain. Quarter the onions and prick a dozen holes in the orange.

Stuff the cavity of the duck with the orange, onion, root ginger, garlic and roast pork. Sew or skewer to make secure.

Put duck in a casserole with 2 pints of water. Place in an oven preheated to 415 degrees. After 15 minutes lower the temperature to 375 degrees.

After 1 hour, skim away any excess fat. Insert cabbage or celery under the duck. Sprinkle with salt. Return the casserole to the oven and continue cooking, at 350 degrees, for another hour. Serve in the casserole.

CLEAR-SIMMERED DUCK WITH ONION AND SPRING GREENS

PREPARATION TIME: 5 minutes. COOKING TIME: 2¼ hours.

1 4–4½ lb duck
4 medium-sized onions
4 hearts of spring greens
1 clove garlic, crushed

½ lb (1 cup) roast pork, both lean and fat (chopped into 1-inch × ½-inch pieces)
2 teaspoons salt

Dip cleaned duck in boiling water for 3 minutes and drain. Quarter each of the onions, remove outer leaves from the greens and cut the hearts into fours.

Stuff the cavity of the duck with onion, garlic and roast pork, adding 1 teaspoon salt. Sew or skewer to make secure. Place in a casserole, add 2 pints water, and put in an oven pre-heated to 415 degrees. After 15 minutes lower the temperature to 375 degrees.

After 1 hour, skim away any excess fat. Place the spring greens underneath the duck. Sprinkle with 1 teaspoon salt. Return the casserole to the oven, lower heat to 350 degrees and cook for another hour. Serve in the casserole.

LONG-SIMMERED DUCK WITH MUSHROOMS AND SHREDDED PORK TOPPING

PREPARATION TIME: 10–12 minutes. COOKING TIME: 2¼ hours.

Follow the previous recipe, but this time stir-fry the stuffing in a mixture of 2 tablespoons soya sauce, 1 teaspoon sugar and 1 tablespoon oil for 3 minutes.

For sauce:

4 tablespoons shredded pork (in thin strips)	1 teaspoon chopped chilli pepper
4 tablespoons shredded mushrooms	1 tablespoon vegetable oil
4 tablespoons chopped spring onion	2 tablespoons soya sauce
	1 teaspoon sugar
	3 tablespoons sherry

When the duck is nearly ready, stir-fry pork, mushrooms, spring onion and chilli pepper in vegetable oil in a small frying-pan, adding soya sauce and sugar, pour over the duck, together with sherry, a minute before serving.

WINE-SIMMERED DUCK

PREPARATION TIME: 5–6 minutes. COOKING TIME: 2 hours.

1 3–4 lb duck
2 medium-sized onions
1 orange
2 pints gunpowder sauce (see pp.19–20)

bouquet garni (2 sachets)
2 tablespoons sugar
1 bottle white wine (hock, graves, moselle, etc)

Dip cleaned duck in boiling water for 3 minutes and drain. Quarter the onions and prick a dozen holes in the orange before packing it into the cavity of the duck along with the onion.

Put the gunpowder sauce, bouquet garni and sugar in a pot large enough to take the duck, and bring to the boil. Immerse the duck in the sauce to simmer gently for 1 hour.

Drain and transfer the duck to a casserole. Pour the wine over the duck, cover the casserole and place in an oven pre-heated to 350 degrees. Cook for 1 hour and serve in the casserole.

EIGHT PRECIOUS DUCK

PREPARATION TIME: 15–20 minutes. COOKING TIME: 2 hours.

Eight Precious Duck is simply either a long-simmered or long-steamed duck stuffed with eight items in varying amounts.

1 4–5 lb duck
1 pint 'broth'

1 teaspoon salt

For stuffing:

cooked rice
green peas
dried mushrooms (optional

but preferable – see p.1),
soaked and chopped into
¼-inch squares

smoked ham

chinese sausages (substitute salami)

dates (remove stones)

dried shrimps (if available)

1 small tin water chestnuts, drained

Mix stuffing ingredients, which should weigh a total of 1½ to 2 lb. When stuffed the bird should be sewn or skewered securely.

Place the duck in a large casserole; pour 'broth' over it and sprinkle with salt.

Cook in an oven preheated to 350 degrees for the first hour, and reduced to 325 degrees for the next 1½ hours.

When served, the stuffing should be scooped out of the cavity and laid as a raised bed in the centre of the serving dish, and the duck flattened out and laid spread-eagled on top of the stuffing.

Leftover Duck

In China many shredded and sliced duck dishes are prepared from cooked duck meat.

Portions: all the following recipes are meant to serve 3–4 people, when eaten with soup, rice and at least 2 other dishes.

ORANGE DUCK

PREPARATION TIME: 5 minutes. COOKING TIME: 7–8 minutes.

Half a roast duck

2 tablespoons vegetable oil

3 stalks spring onion, cut into 1-inch segments

2 slices root ginger (or 3 teaspoons finely chopped

lemon rind shavings)

3 tablespoons gunpowder sauce (see pp.19–20)

2 teaspoons chutney

1 orange for garnish

For sauce:

Juice from 1 orange
1 tablespoon soya sauce
1 teaspoon sugar
2 tablespoons sherry

$\frac{3}{4}$ tablespoon cornflour,
blended in 2 tablespoons
water

First, squeeze the juice from 1 orange and blend with other sauce ingredients into a smooth mixture.

Then chop the duck into 2-inch × 1$\frac{1}{2}$-inch bite-sized pieces. Stir-fry in oil with onion, root ginger and gunpowder sauce for 6–7 minutes over moderate heat. Arrange and reassemble neatly on a serving dish.

Add chutney to the pan, stir-fry in remaining oil for $\frac{1}{4}$ minute. Pour in the sauce mixture. As soon as it thickens pour it over the duck in the dish. Decorate the duck and dish with wedges and thin slices from the orange.

BRAISED DUCK WITH MUSHROOMS

PREPARATION TIME: 5–6 minutes. SOAKING TIME: 30 minutes (for dried mushrooms). COOKING TIME: 8–9 minutes.

6 large dried mushrooms
(optional, but preferable –
see p.1)
6 large mushrooms
Half a roast duck
2 tablespoons vegetable oil
1 clove garlic, chopped
1 tablespoon chopped spring
onion

2 tablespoons gunpowder
sauce (see pp.19–20)
2 tablespoons sherry
$\frac{1}{2}$ cup (mushroom) water
$\frac{3}{4}$ tablespoon cornflour,
blended in 4 tablespoons
'broth' (see pp.18–19)

Soak dried mushrooms in $\frac{1}{4}$ cup warm water for half an hour (retain mushroom water). Cut mushrooms into quarters (remove stems). Chop duck into 2-inch × 1$\frac{1}{2}$-inch bite-sized pieces.

Heat oil in a frying-pan with a lid, or a sauté-pan. Stir-fry garlic, onion and duck in it for 2 minutes. Add gunpowder sauce, sherry, mushroom water. Stir-fry for 2 minutes and push the duck to one side of the pan. Tip the mushrooms into the centre of the pan. Mix with the sauce and allow to simmer gently under cover for 2 minutes. Transfer the pieces of duck to a well-heated dish and arrange nicely. Pour the cornflour mixture over the mushrooms. Stir together over high heat. Ladle the mushrooms over the duck and pour the thickened sauce over them.

BRAISED DUCK WITH YOUNG LEEKS

PREPARATION TIME: 5–6 minutes. COOKING TIME: 8–9 minutes.

Half a roast duck	1 teaspoon salt
4 tablespoons vegetable oil	2 tablespoons sherry
1 clove garlic, chopped	3 tablespoons 'broth' (see
2 stalks spring onion, cut into	pp.18–19)
1-inch segments	2 tablespoons gunpowder
½ lb (2 cups) young leeks, cut	sauce (see pp.19–20)
into 1-inch segments	

Chop duck through bone into 2-inch × 1½-inch bite-sized pieces. Stir-fry in two tablespoons oil with garlic and onion for 1 minute and push to one side of frying-pan.

Pour remaining oil into the centre of the dish. Add leek and stir-fry over high heat for 2 minutes. Sprinkle with salt. Pour the sherry and 'broth' over the leek. Stir-fry for another 1½ minutes, remove and arrange as bed on a well-heated dish.

Bring the duck back into the centre of the pan. Pour the gunpowder sauce over it and stir-fry for 3–4 minutes over high heat; arrange the duck on top of the leeks and serve.

SHREDDED DUCK WITH STIR-FRIED 'HOT' CELERY

PREPARATION TIME: 6–7 minutes. COOKING TIME: 8–9 minutes.

Half a roast duck
2 red chilli peppers (de-seeded and shredded)
½ lb (2 cups) celery (shredded into double-matchstick-size strips)
1 teaspoon salt

2 tablespoons gunpowder sauce (see pp.19–20)
4 tablespoons vegetable oil
4 tablespoons 'broth' (see pp.18–19)
1½ teaspoons sugar
2 tablespoons sherry

Shred duck meat into double-matchstick-sized strips.

Heat 2 tablespoons oil in a frying-pan. Add chilli pepper. Stir-fry for ½ minute. Add celery. Sprinkle with salt and stir-fry over high heat for 3 minutes. Remove and put aside. Pour the remaining oil into the pan. Add shredded duck meat. Sprinkle with gunpowder sauce. Stir for 1 minute. Return celery and chilli pepper to the pan. Sprinkle with sugar, 'broth' and sherry. Stir-fry over high heat for 3 minutes and serve.

SHREDDED DUCK STIR-FRIED WITH SWEET PEPPER AND BEAN-SPROUTS

PREPARATION TIME: 6–7 minutes. COOKING TIME: 6–7 minutes.

Follow the previous recipe eliminating the celery and adding 1 cup spring onion (cut into 1-inch segments), 1 cup sweet pepper (sliced into double-matchstick-sized strips), 1 cup bean-sprouts. Fry the onion first with the chilli pepper, then sweet pepper and then bean-sprouts – the procedure with the shredded duck and 'final stir-fry' being the same as before.

Eggs

Eggs are very much an international dish, and they occupy much the same place in Chinese cooking as in Western cooking. Since the majority of egg dishes can be prepared and cooked in a short time, they fall particularly well within the sphere of quick and easy cooking.

Portions: Unless otherwise noted, the following recipes will serve 3–4 people, when eaten with 1 meat dish, rice and at least 2 other dishes. They are also especially suitable for providing a western snack-type meal for 1–2 people

BASIC CHINESE SCRAMBLED-OMELETTE

We Chinese do not prepare our omelette in the neat parcelled fashion as you do in the West. Because we stir-fry the egg (in this case gently), the result is a cross between a scrambled egg and the western idea of an omelette. Two ingredients are used with great success in our egg dishes – chopped spring onion and sherry. The two generate a 'bouquet' which endows a simple dish with near grandeur by its aromatic appeal.

PREPARATION TIME: 2–3 minutes. COOKING TIME: 3 minutes.

1½ teaspoons salt

3 stalks spring onion, cut into ¼-inch segments

| 6 eggs | ½ small glass of sherry |
| 4 tablespoons lard | 2 tablespoons soya sauce |

Add salt and spring onion to the eggs and beat together for 15 seconds. Heat lard in a large frying-pan over moderate heat. When it has melted pour in the beaten egg. Tilt the handle of the pan so that the egg will flow evenly over the pan. Leave to heat for 1 to 1½ minutes. Lift the sides of the egg so that the remaining liquid part will flow under. When only about 10–15 per cent of the egg is still liquid, stir and turn the egg gently around with a spoon. Pour the sherry into the pan. Stir and turn once more. Dish out on to a well-heated dish and pour 2 tablespoons of good-quality soya sauce over it. Serve to be eaten immediately.

SCRAMBLED-OMELETTE WITH SWEET AND SOUR SAUCE

PREPARATION TIME: 2–3 minutes. COOKING TIME: 3 minutes.

Repeat preceding recipe, adding 4 tablespoons of shredded ham into the beaten eggs. Heat half a cup of sweet and sour sauce (see p.21) and pour it hot over the eggs when serving.

TRIPLE-LAYER SCRAMBLED-OMELETTE WITH SHRIMPS

PREPARATION TIME: 2–3 minutes. COOKING TIME: 6 minutes.

Follow the preceding recipe using 9 eggs instead of 6 and, in addition, ¼ lb of fresh shrimp meat (approximately 1 cup). Divide the stir-frying of the egg into three sessions, each time using ⅓ of the egg and ⅓ of the shrimps. After each frying, stir and turn once; when the egg is about 85 per cent set, sprinkle with sherry and pepper and transfer to a heated serving dish. Repeat again and place the next 'omelette' on top of the first.

Repeat until the third lot of egg is used. Towards the end of the stir-frying of the last 'omelette' pour over it an extra portion of sherry, so that when the last 'omelette' is added on top of the first two, the warm liquid will drip over the whole dish thus enhancing the 'bouquet'. Pour two tablespoons good quality soya sauce over the dish and bring quickly to the table to be consumed at once.

CRAB SCRAMBLED-OMELETTE

Crab 'omelette' is seldom made in more than 1 layer, but a quantity of strong-tasting vegetable ingredients are usually incorporated into the initial frying.

PREPARATION TIME: 2–3 minutes. COOKING TIME: 3 minutes.

1 teaspoon salt
6 eggs
1 small sweet pepper
4 tablespoons lard
1 clove garlic, crushed
3 tablespoons chopped
spring onion

1 slice root ginger, chopped
(or 1 teaspoon finely chopped
lemon-rind shavings)
¼ lb (1 cup) crab-meat
3 tablespoons sherry

Add salt to eggs and beat for 15 seconds. Dice red pepper into ¾-inch squares.

Heat 2 tablespoons lard in a large frying-pan. Add garlic, onion, root ginger and red pepper. Stir-fry together for 1 minute. Add crab-meat, stir and spread out over the pan for 1 minute. Add remaining lard into the pan. When it has melted tilt the handle of the pan, so that the oil will run and cover the pan evenly. Now pour in the egg. Tilt the pan again, so that the egg will also run and cover the pan evenly. Heat for 1 minute or so. When only 10–15 per cent of the egg is still liquid give it a gentle stir and turn over. Pour the sherry over the pan. Give the 'omelette' another gentle turn and scramble. Transfer the contents to a well-heated dish to be served immediately.

VEGETARIAN SCRAMBLED-OMELETTE

PREPARATION TIME: 5–7 minutes. COOKING TIME: 5–6 minutes.

This is a repeat of the previous recipe, using ¾ lb of shredded vegetables (¼ lb or ½ cup of each type, all chopped into matchstick-sized strips) instead of crab-meat. Because of bulk, the vegetables may require 3–4 minutes of stir-frying together, before they are cooked and ready for the egg to be added. The most commonly used vegetables for the purpose are shredded celery, asparagus, sweet pepper, mushrooms, bamboo-shoots, and bean-sprouts. A small amount of sugar and soya sauce may be sprinkled on the shredded vegetable during the stir-frying. As often as not the vegetables are stir-fried separately first, added to the egg when the latter is nearly set, and then scrambled together.

EGG-FLOWER MEAT

Egg-flower Meat, also known as Pine Flower Meat, is a typical Peking dish, where the eggs and shredded meat (pork) are stir-fried separately, and then brought together in a final assembly frying. A small amount of sherry and an even smaller amount of sesame oil (if not available use 2 teaspoons of peanut butter diluted in 2 teaspoons vegetable oil) are added in the assembly frying to seal the unity and contribute to the distinctive flavour of the dish.

PREPARATION TIME: 6–8 minutes. COOKING TIME: 6–7 minutes. SOAKING TIME: 30 minutes (for dried mushrooms).

¼ lb pork (lean)
4 large mushrooms
4 dried mushrooms (optional but preferable – see p.1)
4 tablespoons lard

2 stalks spring onion, cut into 1-inch segments
1½ tablespoons soya sauce
2 tablespoons 'broth' (see pp.18–19)

1 teaspoon sugar	teaspoons peanut butter
½ teaspoon salt	diluted with 2 teaspoons
4 eggs	peanut oil)
1 teaspoon sesame oil (or 2	½ glass sherry

Cut pork and mushrooms into thin strips.

Heat 2 tablespoons lard in a frying-pan. When hot stir-fry onion, pork and mushrooms over high heat for 1 minute. Add soya sauce, 'broth', sugar and salt, and stir-fry together for another minute. Remove pan from heat and keep warm.

Meanwhile, heat the remaining lard in another frying-pan. When hot add the eggs. Heat until nearly set, stir and turn, and break up into small pieces.

Return the pan containing pork mixture over the heat. Add sesame oil to the pan. When hot stir and scramble with the meat, etc, vigorously for ½ minute. Now add the 'omelette-scrambled-egg' from the other pan and pour sherry over the contents. Stir-fry and scramble gently together for ¼ minute and serve.

SOYA-SIMMERED HARD-BOILED EGGS

PREPARATION TIME: 2–3 minutes. COOKING TIME: 25–30 minutes.

'Soya-simmered eggs' are usually prepared when the eggs are cooked together with red-cooked pork during the last stages of cooking the pork. The hard-boiled eggs are inserted into the meat-gravy for 20–30 minutes of slow simmering, during which the eggs are impregnated with the rich brown colour of the gravy. These eggs are often served cold. When the meat is cold it is taken out, carved into neat slices and served with the eggs, which are also cut into thin slices. Arranged nicely on a dish with a pile of golden-crystallized meat jelly (gravy), the eggs and meat form an attractive hors d'oeuvre.

1 panful of red-cooked pork (see pp. 57–8) with gravy	blended in a little pork gravy
1 tablespoon gelatine powder,	6 hard-boiled eggs
	Few sprays of parsley

Heat red-cooked pork together with gelatine mixture and hard-boiled eggs completely immersed in the gravy. Simmer gently for 25 minutes. Remove the eggs from the gravy and leave to cool. Transfer the pork to a basin or large bowl and place in a refrigerator.

When both the eggs and pork have cooled and the gravy of the meat has set into a jelly, skim away the fat formed on top of the gravy. Dig out 5 or 6 spoonfulls of jelly and arrange it down the middle of an oval dish. Slice the meat and place it in a tile-piece fashion on top of the bed of jelly. Slice each egg into about 10 thin slices, and arrange them in two lines beside the meat and gravy. Decorate with parsley and serve.

STEAMED EGGS (BASIC)

Portions: this dish, and its variation, is suitable as the main part of a very light meal for 1–2 people.

PREPARATION TIME: 2–3 minutes. COOKING TIME: 20–25 minutes.

2 eggs	1 pint 'broth' (see pp. 18–19)
1 teaspoon salt	½ tablespoon chopped chives

Beat eggs thoroughly with a fork for 15 seconds. Add salt and 'broth'. Blend together to a very even consistency. Pour the mixture into a large deep-sided heatproof dish. Place in a steamer (or in a large boiler filled with 1½ inches of boiling water and the heatproof dish raised with a few egg-cups), and steam vigorously for 10 minutes and then gently for 10 minutes. Sprinkle with chopped chives and serve.

This dish, the consistency of which is more like a junket than a custard, is more interesting than it sounds and is excellent served with rice. A favourite dish for the aged and invalid.

FANCY STEAMED EGGS

PREPARATION TIME: 3–4 minutes. COOKING TIME: 20–25 minutes.

The basic steamed eggs can be made more elaborate for those who are neither invalids nor aged by adding crab-meat or lobster-meat to the egg and 'broth' before steaming. As soon as the top of the egg becomes firm – which should be after 15 minutes' steaming – sprinkle gently on top some chopped smoked ham, a few well-chosen shrimps or prawns, and a scatter of green peas and chives. These add immensely to colour appeal. When seafoods are used, usually a tablespoon of sherry or white wine is sprinkled over the egg before serving.

Fish

In Chinese cooking we treat fish very similarly to meat. We prepare and cook it in very much the same manner; we red-cook, steam, long-simmer, braise and deep-fry it, but we do not stir-fry it in the vigorous way we often stir-fry meat, as it will break into pieces if treated in this way. When fish is 'quick-fried' it is usually fried statically, or stirred around slowly in ample sauce.

The most important flavouring for fish in Chinese cooking is strong-flavoured vegetables, such as ginger, garlic, onion, chives. A second line of flavouring comes from dried and salted vegetables, which when soaked often carry a much stronger flavour than when they are fresh. With these two types of flavourings together with meats and meat-gravy, soya sauce and other soya-bean products, plus wine, we Chinese are able to make our fish dishes as tasty and succulent as any of our meat dishes, if not more so.

The principal made-up sauces for fish cooking are: 'broth', gunpowder sauce, and wine sediment paste (see pp.18–22).

Since few fish can stand prolonged cooking (there are exceptions), the flavouring of fish is most often achieved through comparatively lengthy marinating and seasoning, and short sharp cooking, such as quick-steaming, deep-frying, quick-frying and braising. Although almost every kind of food can be red-cooked, fish is seldom cooked in the way meat is red-cooked (which is usually to stew it for at least an hour or two). With fish, red-cooking can perhaps more appropriately be called red-braising, with the process seldom taking more than 10–15 minutes, generally less. Because fish needs to be cooked quickly it is a food which falls appropriately within the category of quick and easy cooking.

Portions: all the following recipes are meant for 3–4 people, when served with soup, rice and at least 2 other dishes.

RED-COOKED FISH (WHOLE)

MARINATING TIME: 15 minutes. PREPARATION TIME: 5–6 minutes. COOKING TIME: 25 minutes.

1 2–3 lb fish (carp, mullet, bream, bass, shad, salmon, etc)	3 tablespoons sherry
	6 tablespoons gunpowder sauce (see pp.19–20)
1½ teaspoons salt	4 rashers bacon
½ tablespoon sugar	3 stalks spring onion cut into
1 tablespoon capers, chopped	2-inch segments

Clean fish thoroughly and rub with salt. Mix sugar, capers and sherry with gunpowder sauce, and pour it over the fish laid out in a deep-sided heatproof oval dish. Leave it to soak in the sauce for the next 15 minutes, turning it over every 5 minutes.

Cut two rashers of bacon into ribbons, across lean and fat. When turning the fish around the last time, insert two rashers of bacon underneath the fish. Drape the top of it with remaining bacon and segments of spring onion. Place the dish in a preheated oven at 425 degrees for 15 minutes. Baste the fish (use a few extra spoonfuls of gunpowder sauce if necessary), and reduce the temperature to 375 degrees for another 15 minutes of cooking in the oven. Serve in the original dish.

RED-COOKED FISH (WHOLE) GARNISHED WITH HAM AND VEGETABLES

PREPARATION TIME: 5–6 minutes. COOKING TIME: 20 minutes.

Presuming that there is not a deep-fryer large enough to accommodate the fish, it is best to finish its cooking in an oven.

1 3 lb fish (carp, mullet, bream, bass, shad, salmon, etc)
1½ teaspoons salt

2 tablespoons flour
6 tablespoons vegetable oil
4 rashers bacon

For Sauce and Garnish:

1 heart of spring greens
1 slice ham (about 1½ oz)
4 large mushrooms
2 stalks spring onion, cut into 2-inch segments)
2 tablespoons vegetable oil
8 tablespoons (½ cup)

gunpowder sauce (see pp.19–20)
2 tablespoons sherry
1½ teaspoons sugar
1 tablespoon cornflour, blended in 3 tablespoons 'broth' (see pp.18–19)

Clean fish thoroughly. Rub with salt and flour. Heat oil in a roasting-pan. Line it with rashers of bacon. Lay the fish on top of the bacon to fry for 2–3 minutes over moderate heat. Turn the fish over and baste well with hot oil, using a large metal spoon. Insert the roasting-pan into an oven preheated to 450 degrees.

Meanwhile slice spring greens, ham and mushrooms into thin strips, and stir-fry them together with onion in 2 tablespoons of oil for 1½ minutes. Add the gunpowder sauce, sherry and sugar. Allow the vegetables and ham to simmer in the sauce and gravy for 3 minutes. Add the cornflour mixture to thicken.

When the fried fish has been in the hot oven for 10 minutes it should begin to be crispy. Transfer the fish with aid of fish-

slice and fork carefully on to a well-heated oval dish. Pour the
sauce over the length of the fish and garnish with ham and
vegetables from the sauce.

SWEET AND SOUR CARP

PREPARATION TIME: 3–4 minutes. COOKING TIME: 24 minutes.

Although it might be best to deep-fry the whole fish, the cooking can be done partly in a hot oven as in the previous recipe.

1 3–4 lb carp
1½ teaspoons salt
3 tablespoons flour
9 tablespoons vegetable oil
4 rashers bacon

1 red or green pepper (sliced
into strips)
1 cup sweet and sour sauce
(see p.21)

Clean fish thoroughly and rub with salt and flour both inside
and out. Heat 8 tablespoons oil in a roasting-pan. Line it with
bacon and place the fish on top; cook over moderate heat for
4–5 minutes. Turn fish over and baste with hot oil for 3–4
minutes. Place the roasting-pan in an oven preheated to 450
degrees.

Meanwhile prepare the pepper and stir-fry in 1 tablespoon
oil for 2 minutes. Add the sweet and sour sauce to heat and
simmer gently together.

When fish is ready (after 12 minutes in the oven), transfer to
a well-heated oval dish. Pour the sauce over the length of the
fish and arrange the pepper strips on top.

RED-COOKED FISH STEAKS

PREPARATION TIME: 3–4 minutes. COOKING TIME: 7–8 minutes.

2 lb fish steaks (cod, halibut,
haddock)
1 teaspoon salt

1 egg
4 tablespoons flour
4 tablespoons water

4 tablespoons vegetable oil
1 clove garlic, crushed
2 stalks spring onion, cut into
1-inch segments

½ pint gunpowder sauce (see
pp.19–20)
½ tablespoon cornflour,
blended in 2 tablespoons
water

Cut fish into 2-inch squares. Mix salt, egg, flour, water into a light batter. Dip the pieces of fish in the batter.

Heat oil in a frying-pan. Stir-fry garlic and onion together for 15 seconds. Push to one side. Add the pieces of fish one by one, laying them down gently into the oil in the pan. Fry over moderate heat, turning the fish over after 1 minute. After another minute's frying, pour ½ the gunpowder sauce over the fish and simmer together for 3 minutes.

Baste fish with the sauce in the pan for 1 minute. Transfer to a well-heated dish and keep hot in the oven. Meanwhile, add remaining gunpowder sauce and cornflour mixture into the pan. Stir until the mixture thickens. Pour this sauce over the fish and serve at once.

PLAIN SALTED DOUBLE-FRIED FISH STEAKS

PREPARATION TIME: 4–5 minutes. COOKING TIME: 5–6 minutes.
SALTING: 30 minutes.

2 lb fish steaks (cod, halibut,
haddock)
3 teaspoons salt
1 egg
4 tablespoons flour
4 tablespoons water
oil for deep-frying

2 stalks spring onion, cut into
1-inch segments
1 clove garlic, crushed
3 tablespoons vegetable oil
2 slices root ginger (or 1
tablespoon finely chopped
lemon-rind shavings)
parsley

Clean fish thoroughly, rub with 2 teaspoons salt, and let stand for half an hour.

Cut fish into 2-inch squares. Mix remaining salt, egg, flour and water into a light batter. Dip the pieces of fish into the batter and deep-fry for 3 minutes.

Remove the fish and keep it hot.

Meanwhile, fry the onion and garlic in 3 tablespoons oil for 1 minute. Add the pieces of fish to the onion and garlic-impregnated oil together with two slices root ginger (or 1 tablespoon finely chopped lemon-rind shavings). Turn the fish over once and serve on a well-heated dish, piled up like a pyramid, topped with a few sprays of parsley.

Fish so cooked is best eaten dipped in tomato sauce, chilli sauce, or just plain.

FISH STEAKS IN SWEET AND SOUR SAUCE

PREPARATION TIME: 5–7 minutes. COOKING TIME: 5–6 minutes.

Use the same amount of fish steaks as in the 2 previous recipes, as well as the same batter. Either deep-fry them for 3 minutes and drain, or pan-fry them (in 6 tablespoons vegetable oil for 2 minutes on each side).

Meanwhile, make up the basic recipe for sweet and sour sauce (see p.21) and pour it over the fish steaks, arranged on a well-heated dish.

FISH STEAKS IN WINE SEDIMENT PASTE

PREPARATION TIME: 2–3 minutes. COOKING TIME: 4–5 minutes.

2 lb fish steaks (cod, halibut, haddock)
4 tablespoons vegetable oil
1 clove garlic (chopped)
2 stalks spring onion (chopped)
6 tablespoons wine sediment paste (see p.p21–2)

For Batter:

1 teaspoon salt
1 egg
4 tablespoons flour
4 tablespoons water

Cut fish into 2-inch squares. Mix batter ingredients into a thin batter. Dip fish in it.

Heat 3 tablespoons oil in a frying-pan. Fry garlic and onion for $\frac{1}{2}$ minute and push to one side. Lay the pieces of fish on to the hot oil to fry for $1\frac{1}{2}$ minutes on each side, basting as you go along. Add remaining oil and wine sediment paste to the centre of the pan. Stir until they are well blended.

Turn the pieces of fish in the wine sediment sauce for a minute until each piece is well covered. Serve by arranging the pieces nicely on a well-heated dish, topped with this sauce.

LONG-SIMMERED FISH IN VINEGAR SAUCE

PREPARATION TIME: 5–6 minutes. COOKING TIME: $3\frac{1}{2}$–4 hours.

This is one of the few occasions where the fish is subjected to prolonged cooking.

6 small carp (or fat herrings or eel segments), about $2\frac{1}{2}$ lb	into strips)
6 rashers bacon	1 tablespoon chopped lemon rind
2 cloves garlic, crushed	6 tablespoons wine vinegar
1 onion, sliced	6 tablespoons gunpowder
$\frac{1}{2}$ tablespoon sugar	sauce (see pp.19–20)
1 chilli pepper (sliced into strips)	2 tablespoons soya sauce
	2 tablespoons sherry
1 red or green pepper (sliced	8 tablespoons red wine

Place the fish and bacon in alternate layers at the bottom of a casserole, starting with 3 rashers of bacon. Scatter the garlic, onion, sugar, pepper and lemon rind evenly over the fish and pour in all the liquid ingredients. Add water to cover the fish by $\frac{1}{2}$ inch. Bring the contents to boil and insert the casserole into an oven preheated to 325 degrees. Cook for 1 hour under firm cover and then reduce to 290 degrees for $2\frac{1}{2}$–3 more hours.

By the end of the cooking even the bones of the fish should be soft enough to eat!

CLEAR-SIMMERED FISH (WHOLE)

PREPARATION TIME: 3–4 minutes. COOKING TIME: 20 minutes.
SALTING: 10 minutes.

1 2–3 lb fish (sole, mullet, bream, bass, etc)
2 teaspoons salt
2 stalks young leeks, cut into 3-inch segments

1 cup 'broth' (see pp.18–19)
1½ teaspoons sugar
2 tablespoons sherry
1 clove garlic, chopped
1 teaspoon lemon juice

Clean fish thoroughly, rub with salt, and leave to stand for 10 minutes. Prepare leek and place in the bottom of a roasting-pan. Place the fish on top and pour in the 'broth'. Bring to boil quickly on top of stove. Remove from heat and cover the top of the pan firmly with a sheet of foil. Place the pan in an oven, preheated to 425 degrees, for 5 minutes and reduce to 375 degrees for another 8–10 minutes. Transfer the fish to a deep-sided oval serving dish. Add sugar, sherry and garlic into the roasting-pan. Stir over high heat for ¼ minute. Pour this sauce over the fish and squeeze lemon juice over the top. The sauce, which is half soup, half gravy, is excellent with rice.

CLEAR-SIMMERED FISH (WHOLE) WITH SHREDDED PORK AND MUSHROOM TOPPING

PREPARATION TIME: 3–4 minutes. COOKING TIME: 20 minutes.

Follow the preceding recipe but rub the fish with only 1½ teaspoons salt. Prepare the following topping in a separate pan:

For sauce:

1 cup shredded pork
½ cup shredded mushrooms
2 stalks spring onion, cut into 1-inch segments

2 tablespoons oil
3 tablespoons gunpowder sauce
½ teaspoon salt

1 teaspoon sugar tablespoon finely chopped
pepper lemon-rind shavings)
1 slice ginger root (or ½ 4–5 tablespoons fish stock

Quick-fry pork, mushrooms and spring onion in oil for 5 minutes; add remaining ingredients. Pour the resultant sauce over the fish.

CLEAR-SIMMERED FISH (WHOLE) WITH HOT SAUCE

PREPARATION TIME: 3–4 minutes. COOKING TIME: 20 minutes.

1 2–3 lb fish (sole, mullet, 3 stalks young leeks, cut into
bream, bass, etc) 3-inch segments
2 teaspoons salt 1 cup 'broth' see(pp.18–19)

For sauce:

1 green pepper, thinly sliced 4 tablespoons gunpowder
1 or 2 chilli peppers, thinly sauce (see pp.19–20)
sliced 3 tablespoons fish stock
2 tablespoons vegetable oil 1 teaspoon lemon juice

Clean fish thoroughly, rub with salt and leave to stand for 10 minutes. Prepare leeks and place in a roasting-pan. Put the fish on top and pour in the 'broth'.

Quickly bring to boil on top of stove. Remove from heat and cover pan firmly with a sheet of foil. Insert in an oven, preheated to 425 degrees for 5 minutes, reduce temperature to 375 degrees and cook for another 8–10 minutes.

Meanwhile, heat oil in a frying-pan and stir-fry the green pepper, 1 or 2 chilli peppers (depending on how hot you want the dish) and capers. After 1 minute add remaining ingredients and continue to stir-fry for another minute.

Remove the fish to a serving dish, pour the hot sauce over it and decorate with the red and green pepper strips.

DOUBLE-FRIED EEL

PREPARATION TIME: 4–5 minutes. COOKING TIME: 12–15 minutes.

1 3–4 lb eel
oil for deep-frying
2 tablespoons lard
1 clove garlic, chopped
2 stalks spring onion, cut into
1-inch segments
½ tablespoon finely chopped
lemon-rind shavings

2 stalks young leeks, cut into
1-inch segments
1 teaspoon salt
2 tablespoons gunpowder
sauce (see pp.19–20)
2 tablespoons wine sediment
paste (see pp.21–2)
2 tablespoons sherry

Chop eel into 3-inch segments. Dip in boiling water for 1 minute. Drain and dry. Deep-fry in hot oil for 5 minutes. Scrape off all the meat without breaking it into too small pieces. Deep-fry the eel meat, using a wire-basket, for another 2½ minutes in very hot oil. Drain thoroughly.

Meanwhile, heat lard in a frying-pan. Add garlic, onion, lemon rind, leek and salt. Stir-fry for 1 minute, add gunpowder sauce, wine sediment paste, and sherry. Stir-fry for half-minute.

Add all the eel. Turn it in the sauce for 1 minute and serve. This is a favourite dish from Shanghai.

Steamed Fish

Steaming is a common Chinese method of cooking fish. For the best results fish should be salted, seasoned, and marinated for 15 minutes or more and then subjected to a short sharp period of steaming of about 15–20 minutes (depending on size).

STEAMED SOLE WITH BACON AND MUSHROOM GARNISH

PREPARATION TIME: 3–4 minutes. SOAKING TIME: 20 minutes (for dried mushrooms). COOKING TIME: 15–16 minutes.

1 fat sole, about 2–3 lb
1 teaspoon salt
3 tablespoons gunpowder sauce (see pp.19–20)
2 tablespoons chopped onion
1 clove garlic, crushed

2 stalks spring onion, cut into 2-inch segments
2 large mushrooms (preferably dried – see p.1)
2 rashers bacon
3 tablespoons sherry

Clean fish thoroughly and rub with salt, gunpowder sauce, chopped onion and garlic. Leave to marinate for 15 minutes.

Prepare spring onion and slice mushrooms into similarly sized strips. Slice bacon across lean and fat into similar strips.

Place fish in an oval or oblong-shaped heatproof dish. Garnish with spring onion, mushroom and bacon. Pour the remaining marinade over the length of the fish. Place the fish in a steamer for 15 minutes' vigorous steaming. Serve in the original dish.

STEAMED FISH WITH SHREDDED PORK GARNISH AND HOT SAUCE

PREPARATION TIME: 3–4 minutes. COOKING TIME: 15–16 minutes.

For sauce:

3–4 oz (approximately $\frac{1}{2}$ cup) shredded pork
1 red or green pepper (shredded)

1 tablespoon chopped capers
1$\frac{1}{2}$ teaspoons chilli sauce
4 tablespoons gunpowder sauce (see pp.19–20)

½ tablespoon finely chopped   1 tablespoon soya sauce
lemon-rind shavings   2 tablespoons sherry
1 tablespoon tomato sauce   2 tablespoons vegetable oil

Using sole, mullet, bream, etc, proceed according to the preceding recipe, but do not garnish the fish before steaming. Steam the fish for 15–20 minutes (20 minutes if over 2½ lb) directly after seasoning.

Meanwhile, stir-fry all the above ingredients in oil for 3 minutes over high heat. Pour the sauce over the length of the fish immediately on removing it from the steamer, and serve in the original dish.

CASSEROLE OF FISH STEAKS IN TOMATO SAUCE

PREPARATION TIME: 3–4 minutes. COOKING TIME: 10 minutes.

2 lb fish steaks   6 medium-sized tomatoes
1½ teaspoons salt   4 tablespoons gunpowder
1 tablespoon flour   sauce (see pp. 19–20)
3 tablespoons vegetable oil   2 tablespoons sherry
1 onion, chopped   ¾ tablespoon cornflour,
1 clove garlic, chopped   blended in 6 tablespoons
1 tablespoon chopped capers   'broth' (see pp. 18–19)

Cut fish into 2-inch square pieces. Rub with salt and flour. Heat oil in flameproof casserole. Add onion, garlic, capers. Stir-fry for ½ minute. Add fish. Fry for 1 minute on each side, remove with perforated spoon and put aside.

Meanwhile, skin the tomatoes (this is made easier by first dipping them into boiling water). Cut each into half and place in the casserole to fry in the remaining oil over high heat for 1 minute.

Add the gunpowder sauce. Stir-fry for 1 minute. Add sherry and the cornflour mixture. Stir until the sauce is smooth and thickened. Place the fish in the casserole, carefully coating each piece in sauce. Close the casserole with a lid, and allow it to simmer over low heat for 4–5 minutes; serve in the casserole.

CASSEROLE OF FISH STEAKS WITH MUSHROOMS

PREPARATION TIME: 2–3 minutes. COOKING TIME 10 minutes.
SOAKING TIME: 30 minutes (for dried mushrooms).

6 large dried mushrooms
(optional but preferable – see
p.1)
2 lb fish steaks
1½ teaspoons salt
1 tablespoon flour
3 tablespoons vegetable oil
1 onion, chopped
1 clove garlic, chopped

1 tablespoon chopped capers
6 large mushrooms
oil for frying
3 teaspoons cornflour
(blended in ½ cup 'broth' – see
pp.18–19)
2 tablespoons sherry
1 teaspoon salt
½ cup (mushroom) water

If using dried mushrooms, retain the water in which they are
soaked.

Cut fish into 2-inch square pieces. Rub with salt and flour.
Heat 3 tablespoons oil in flameproof casserole. Stir-fry onion,
garlic and capers for ½ minute. Add fish, fry for 1 minute on
each side, remove with a perforated spoon and put aside.

Remove the stems from mushrooms and cut into halves.
Fry them in oil over moderate heat for 1½ minutes. Pour in
cornflour mixture, sherry, salt and ½ cup (mushroom) water.
Stir until the liquid reboils and thickens. Return the fish to the
casserole. Spread it out, and spoon some mushrooms and soup
over each piece of fish. Close the lid of the casserole and cook
over low heat for 5 minutes; serve in the casserole.

CASSEROLE OF FISH STEAKS WITH WATERCRESS, PARSLEY, PICKLES AND SALTED VEGETABLES

PREPARATION TIME: 2–3 minutes. COOKING TIME: 10 minutes.

2 lb fish steaks
1½ teaspoons salt
1 tablespoon flour
3 tablespoons vegetable oil

1 onion, chopped
1 clove garlic, chopped
1 tablespoon chopped capers

For sauce:

1 tablespoon capers, chopped
2 tablespoons chopped
chutney
2 tablespoons sliced
gherkins
3 tablespoons parsley,
chopped coarsely

3 tablespoons watercress
oil for frying
1 cup 'broth' (see pp.18–19)
4 tablespoons sherry
1 tablespoon soya sauce
½ teaspoon salt

Follow directions for preparing fish in previous recipe to the point where the fish is removed after the initial frying.

Add capers, chutney, gherkins, parsley and watercress to stir-fry for 1 minute in oil. Pour in 'broth' and sherry; add soya sauce and salt. Return fish to the casserole. Spread the pieces out. Heat until the liquid boils. Close the lid, simmer for 5 minutes over low heat and serve in the casserole.

STUFFED FISH SIMMERED IN WINE

PREPARATION TIME: 5–6 minutes. COOKING TIME: 35 minutes.

1 large fish (4–5 lb carp,
bream, mullet, bass, salmon)
2 teaspoons salt
3 tablespoons flour
½ lb (approximately 1 cup)
roast pork, Chinese or
western, (cut into 1-inch ×
½-inch pieces)
6 stalks spring onion, cut

into 1-inch segments
2 cloves garlic, crushed
¼ pint vegetable oil for semi-
deep-frying
2 cups 'broth' (see pp.18–19)
2 cups white wine (dry)
4 tablespoons gunpowder
sauce (see pp.19–20)
2 teaspoons sugar

Clean and rub fish with salt and flour. Stuff cavity with pork and spring onion, and garlic. Skewer or sew to secure.

Heat oil in an oval-shaped casserole. When very hot lower fish to fry in it for 5 minutes. Baste continually, turning the fish over once. Drain away all the oil.

Pour into the casserole, 'broth', wine and gunpowder sauce and sugar. Bring to gentle boil. Close the lid of the casserole and simmer for ½ hour. Serve in the casserole.

STUFFED FISH SIMMERED IN WINE AND VINEGAR SAUCE

PREPARATION TIME: 5–6 minutes. COOKING TIME: 35 minutes.

2 1–2 lb fish (small carp, mullet, or large herring)
1½ teaspoons salt
3 tablespoons flour
4 stalks spring onion, cut into 1-inch segments)
2 cloves garlic, crushed
4 tablespoons smoked ham
4 tablespoons smoked haddock

4 tablespoons mussels (fresh) or oysters
½ pint oil for semi-deep-frying
2 stalks young leeks, cut into 1-inch segments
1 cup 'broth' (see pp.18–19)
1 cup white wine (dry)
4 tablespoons wine vinegar
1 tablespoon soya sauce

Clean the fish thoroughly and rub fish, inside and out, with salt and flour. Combine the onion, garlic, ham, haddock and mussels, and stuff this mixture into the cavities of the fish. Sew or skewer to secure.

Heat oil in a casserole. Lower the fish to fry in the oil over moderate heat for 4–5 minutes. Drain away all the oil. Place the leek underneath the fish. Pour in the 'broth', wine, vinegar and soya sauce. Bring to boil and simmer gently for 30 minutes. Serve in the casserole.

FOUR TREASURE STUFFED SIMMERED FISH

PREPARATION TIME: 7–8 minutes. COOKING TIME: 35 minutes.

Follow the directions in the preceding recipe, stuffing the fish with 4 tablespoons diced cooked chicken, 4 tablespoons diced

mushrooms, 4 tablespoons diced ham, 6 tablespoons cooked
rice – and without use of vinegar in the simmering.

Quick-fried Sliced Fish

Sliced fish differs from fish steaks in that it is always very thinly
sliced (to about ⅛–¼ inch thick) which makes it possible to cook
in an instant. It is almost always 'wet quick-fried', that is quick-
fried in sauce. The operation is a very delicate one because the
pieces of fish are so thin that they break up into unsightly
pieces very easily. Therefore, only very firm and fresh fish can
be used for this type of cooking.

SLICED FISH QUICK-FRIED IN WINE SAUCE

PREPARATION TIME: 4–5 minutes. COOKING TIME: 2–3 minutes.

1¼ lb very fresh filleted fish
(sole, halibut, carp, etc)
1 teaspoon salt
1 egg white
2 tablespoons cornflour
4 tablespoons vegetable oil
1 tablespoon finely chopped
onion
1 slice root ginger (or 2

teaspoons finely chopped
lemon-rind shavings)
4 tablespoons white wine
(dry)
1 tablespoon cornflour,
blended in 6 tablespoons
'broth' (see pp. 18–19)
1½ teaspoons sugar

Cut fish with sharp knife into thin slices, approximately
2 inches × 1 inch, and rub with salt. Beat egg white for 30
seconds with a rotary beater. Dip fish in egg white and dust
lightly with cornflour.

Heat oil in a frying-pan over moderate heat. Fry onion and
ginger in it for half a minute. Lay the pieces of sliced fish carefully in the oil to fry gently for ¾ minute on each side. Remove
with a fish-slice and keep hot.

Drain away any excess oil in the pan. Add wine, cornflour

mixture and sugar. Stir until the sauce thickens. Return the pieces of sliced fish to the pan. Spread them out and turn them in the sauce for 1 minute. Serve on a well-heated dish; to be eaten immediately.

SLICED FISH QUICK-FRIED IN SWEET AND SOUR SAUCE

PREPARATION TIME: 4–5 minutes. COOKING TIME: 2–3 minutes.

Follow the preceding recipe, substituting 8 tablespoons sweet and sour sauce (see p.21) for wine/cornflour mixture, adding 1 tablespoon sweet pickles into the frying just before adding the sweet and sour sauce into the pan, and 2 tablespoons of sherry after the fish has been introduced into the sauce for the final assembly frying.

SLICED FISH QUICK-FRIED IN WINE SEDIMENT PASTE

PREPARATION TIME: 4–5 minutes. COOKING TIME: 2–3 minutes.

Follow the recipe for Sliced Fish Quick-fried in Wine Sauce, substituting 6 tablespoons wine sediment paste and ½ tablespoon cornflour blended with 'broth', for the white wine, and larger cornflour/'broth' mixture in the final assembly frying.

TOASTED FISH

PREPARATION TIME: 5–6 minutes. COOKING TIME: 2–3 minutes.

2 eggs
½ teaspoon salt
4 slices bread
1 lb filleted fish

¼ lb (1 cup) breadcrumbs
oil for deep-frying
2 tablespoons coarsely
chopped parsley

Beat eggs and salt with a rotary whisk for 15 seconds. Cut away the crust from the bread, and cut each piece into six. Slice fish into 24 pieces, approximately the same size as the pieces of bread. Spread half the breadcrumbs on a large plate or tray.

Dip the fish and bread quickly in the beaten egg to give a light coating. Place the pieces of fish on top of the bread pieces, pressing them lightly together. Put the miniature 'open sandwiches' on the breadcrumbs spread out on the tray and sprinkle each heavily with additional breadcrumbs. Proceed until all the pieces of fish and bread are used up and formed into breadcrumbed canapés.

Heat oil in a deep-fryer. When very hot place canapés, 6 at a time, in a wire-basket and deep-fry for approximately $2\frac{1}{2}$ minutes. You will note that as soon as the canapé is sunk in the hot oil it becomes one firm piece. When all the pieces have been fried, arrange them nicely on a well-heated serving dish, place a pinch of chopped parsley on top of each piece and serve. An appealing dish, particularly for a cocktail party.

Seafood and Shell Fish

Since the cross-cooking and cross-blending of flavours are very much in the tradition of Chinese cooking, seafoods are often used primarily for flavouring. In this section, however, we shall deal with them mainly when they are used as the principal material in a dish, or at least provide the principal flavour.

Portions: as usual, the following recipes are meant to serve 3–4 people, when eaten with rice and at least 2 other dishes.

Abalone

This rubbery textured seafood is used much more often as a flavouring than as the main ingredient of a dish, but it figures in a number of combination dishes. Like most seafood abalone requires very little cooking.

ABALONE QUICK-FRIED WITH MUSHROOMS AND BROCCOLI

PREPARATION TIME: 5–6 minutes. SOAKING TIME: 20 minutes (for dried mushrooms). COOKING TIME: 3–4 minutes.

1 tin abalone (approximately 10 oz)
½ tablespoon cornflour, blended in 4 tablespoons

abalone water
6 large dried mushrooms (optional but preferable – see p.1)

6 large mushrooms
¼ lb (1 cup) broccoli, chopped into 1½-inch × 1-inch pieces
2 tablespoons vegetable oil
1 tablespoon chopped onion

1 clove garlic, chopped
4 tablespoons gunpowder sauce (see pp.19–20)
1 tablespoon soya sauce
1 tablespoon sherry
3 tablespoons (mushroom) water

Slice the abalone into approximately 2 × 1 × ½-inch pieces. Retain abalone water, and blend with cornflour. (If using dried mushrooms, retain 3 tablespoons of the water in which they are soaked.) De-stem mushrooms and cut into quarters. Parboil broccoli for 3 minutes.

Heat oil in a frying-pan. When hot add onion and garlic. Stir-fry over moderate heat for ½ minute. Add broccoli and mushrooms and stir-fry together for 1½ minutes. Add sliced abalone and gunpowder sauce and stir-fry for a further minute. Finally, add cornflour mixture, soya sauce, sherry and 3 tablespoons mushroom water. Stir until sauce thickens. Serve on a well-heated dish.

ABALONE QUICK-FRIED WITH SLICED CHICKEN AND MUSHROOMS

PREPARATION TIME: 5–6 minutes. SOAKING TIME: 20 minutes (for dried mushrooms). COOKING TIME: 3–4 minutes.

Follow the preceding recipe, substituting sliced chicken (one whole breast of chicken sliced to the same size as the abalone) for broccoli. Add the chicken, together with abalone and mushrooms, immediately after the garlic and onion has been fried for ½ minute, and stir-fry together for 1½ minutes before adding the gunpowder sauce for ½ minute's stir-fry. A dash of chilli sauce may be introduced here before adding the blended cornflour mixture for the final assembly frying.

ABALONE WITH CHOPPED RED-COOKED PORK

PREPARATION TIME: 3–4 minutes. COOKING TIME: 3–4 minutes.

1 tin abalone (about 10 oz)
1 tablespoon cornflour,
blended in 6 tablespoons
abalone water
2 lb Red-cooked Pork with
gravy (see pp.57–8. In the

present case it is the abalone
which is emphasized, rather
than the pork which is taken
as ready cooked)
2 tablespoons sherry

Cut abalone into 2- × 1- × ½-inch slices. Retain water and blend
with cornflour.

Heat pork and gravy, together with abalone, in a saucepan.
When hot add the cornflour mixture and sherry. Simmer together for 3 minutes and serve in a bowl or deep-sided
dish.

Clams

CLAMS SIMMERED IN CLEAR CONSOMMÉ

PREPARATION TIME: 5–6 minutes. COOKING TIME: 5–6 minutes.

8 clams
1 breast of chicken
1 teaspoon salt

½ pint 'broth' (see pp.18–19)
2 tablespoons sherry

Shell clams. Remove impurities and intestines, leaving only the
white meat. Cut into 2–3 slices. Cut chicken into similar sizes.

Heat ½ pint water in a frying-pan. Add salt and chicken. Simmer gently for 3 minutes. Skim away any impurities and pour
away half the water. Add 'broth', sherry and clams. Simmer
them together for 2½ minutes. Sprinkle with chopped chives
and serve.

Clams cooked lightly in this manner should be eaten dipped in good-quality soya sauce, soya-chilli dip, soya-vinegar dip or soya-sherry dip (see p.85) and tomato sauce – which should all be placed on sauce dishes at strategic points on the dining-table.

STUFFED DEEP-FRIED CLAMS

PREPARATION TIME: 7–8 minutes. COOKING TIME: 9–10 minutes.

6 clams
¼ lb lean and fat pork
1 egg
1 teaspoon salt
2 tablespoons finely chopped onion

1 tablespoon flour
1 clove garlic, crushed
a dash of cinnamon
oil for deep-frying
parsley

Clean the clams as directed in the previous recipe, reserving the half-shells. Poach the clam meat in boiling water, simmering for 1½ minutes. Drain and reduce in a mincer into a fine mince. Simultaneously, boil pork vigorously for 5 minutes and reduce to similar fine-grain mince. Mix the two minces together with the next 6 ingredients, into a consistent paste. Stuff the paste into the 12 half-shells.

Heat the oil in the deep-fryer to a high temperature. Lower 6 stuffed half-shells at a time to deep-fry for 3½–4 minutes. Keep very hot. When all the 12 stuffed half-shells are ready, arrange on a heatproof dish. Decorate with sprigs of parsley, and serve. The dish should be eaten accompanied by the same dips as in the previous recipe.

Crab

An enormous quantity of crab is eaten in China, either cooked in the shell or the crab-meat extracted and cooked with other materials.

QUICK-FRIED CRAB WITH EGG SAUCE

PREPARATION TIME: 4–5 minutes. COOKING TIME: 8–9 minutes.

2 large crabs
3 tablespoons vegetable oil
2 tablespoons chopped
onion
2 cloves garlic, chopped

1 tablespoon chopped capers
1 teaspoon salt
2 teaspoons vinegar
1 tablespoon sherry

For Egg Sauce:

2 egg yolks
4 tablespoons water
1 tablespoon cornflour

½ cup 'broth' (see pp.18–19)
½ teaspoon salt

Remove top shells of crabs. Chop body into 6 pieces, each piece with leg or claw attached. Chop shell into two, and crack claws slightly with back of chopper.

Beat egg yolks and water together for 15 seconds. Blend cornflour with 'broth' and salt. Heat the latter mixture in a small pan until the sauce is smooth and thickens. Stream in the egg-yolk mixture slowly in a very thin stream, forming a cloud effect in the sauce. Stir and remove from heat.

Heat oil in a large frying-pan. Stir-fry onion, garlic, and capers in it for ½ minute. Add the chopped crab, sprinkle with salt and stir-fry over high heat for 2½ minutes. Stream the egg sauce over the crab, especially over the meatier parts. Add vinegar and sherry. Lower the heat, place the lid on the pan, and allow contents to simmer for 2–3 minutes. Serve immediately. (The great pleasure and taste in eating this dish lies in sucking the meat and sauce out of the body of the crab, holding on to its leg or claw. The latter is cracked open and eaten last.)

The only traditional sauce used on the table for dipping is *ginger and vinegar mix*: 1 tablespoon shredded root ginger mixed with 3–4 tablespoons vinegar; or 1 tablespoon chopped dried ginger soaked in 4 tablespoons vinegar.

DEEP-FRIED CRAB

PREPARATION TIME: 4–5 minutes. COOKING TIME: 8–9 minutes.

2–3 crabs (medium to large   oil for deep-frying
size)

For Batter:

1 egg   1 clove garlic, crushed
3 tablespoons flour   1 tablespoon chopped spring
4 tablespoons water   onion
1 teaspoon salt

Steam the crabs vigorously for 5 minutes by placing them in a
heatproof basin, and lowering the basin into a large boiler or
saucepan containing $1\frac{1}{2}$ inches boiling water. Close the lid and
keep water at a rolling boil for 5–6 minutes.

Remove the top shells from the crabs and chop body into
4–6 pieces, each piece with a leg or claw attached. Crack the
claw slightly with a rolling-pin or back of chopper.

Mix the ingredients for the batter together. Dip the meat end
of the pieces of crab in the batter. Heat the oil in the deep-fryer
and deep-fry the pieces of crab (including shell) in two lots
for $3\frac{1}{2}$–4 minutes each. Serve by arranging the pieces and shells
nicely on a well-heated dish.

Deep-fried Crab can be eaten with the fingers, holding on to
the legs and claws and dipped in ginger-vinegar dip, or any of
the dips used for Clams simmered in Clear Consommé (see
pp.144–5).

GRILLED CRAB

PREPARATION TIME: 4–5 minutes. COOKING TIME: 8–9 minutes.

Crabs prepared in the same manner as in the preceding recipe
can also be grilled or barbecued. To grill, the crab should be

dipped in batter and placed under the grill at high heat for 2½ minutes on either side. An added refinement is for the pieces of crab to be brushed lightly with onion-impregnated oil (simmer 2 tablespoons onion in 3 tablespoons oil for 3 minutes) before being dipped in batter.

QUICK-FRIED CRAB-MEAT WITH PORK AND EGGS

PREPARATION TIME: 4–5 minutes. COOKING TIME: 4–5 minutes.

¾ lb crab-meat
4 eggs
2 tablespoons lard
¼ lb minced pork
1 clove garlic, chopped
1 tablespoon chopped onion

1 teaspoon salt
1 tablespoon soya sauce
2 tablespoons sherry
¾ teaspoon sugar
2 stalks spring onion, cut into 1-inch segments

Shred crab-meat, beat eggs lightly. Heat lard in a frying-pan. Add pork, garlic and chopped onion. Sprinkle with salt. Stir-fry together over high heat for 2 minutes. Add crab-meat. Sprinkle with soya sauce, half the sherry and sugar and stir-fry together for 1 minute. Add spring onion and pour in the eggs. As soon as they begin to set, sprinkle with remaining sherry. Stir and scramble the egg and crab together lightly and serve.

Lobster

In Chinese cuisine lobster is treated very similarly to crab and can be cooked in most of the ways that crab is (the difference being mainly one of shape). In China lobsters are treated with a little more respect because of their comparative rarity. They are called 'dragon shrimps'.

LOBSTER AND PORK IN EGG SAUCE

PREPARATION TIME: 4–5 minutes. COOKING TIME: 6–7 minutes.

1 1½–2 lb lobster
3 tablespoons vegetable oil
1 clove garlic, chopped
2 tablespoons chopped
spring onion
¼ lb lean pork, minced

½ teaspoon salt
2 tablespoons soya sauce
2 slices chopped root ginger
(or 1 tablespoon finely
chopped lemon-rind
shavings)

For the Egg Sauce:

2 eggs
½ teaspoon salt
¼ cup water
1 tablespoon cornflour

½ cup 'broth' (see pp. 18–19)
3 tablespoons sherry
1 teaspoon sugar

After cleaning thoroughly cut lobster lengthwise with sharp chopper, and then cut into segments of about 1½ inches. Crack the claws.

Heat oil in a heavy saucepan. Stir-fry garlic and onion over high heat for half a minute. Add pork and stir-fry for 1 minute. Add the lobster segments. Sprinkle with salt and continue to stir-fry for 1½ minutes. Add soya sauce and ginger.

Meanwhile, beat eggs and blend with salt and water. Blend cornflour with cold 'broth', sherry, and sugar. Pour the cornflour mixture into the pan. Stir the lobster in the sauce. Lower the heat slightly and pour the egg/water mixture, in a thin stream, evenly over lobster segments and sauce. Stir the contents of the pan around once. Close the lid of the pan, allow the contents to simmer for 2 minutes and serve in a well-heated deep-sided dish.

BAKED LOBSTER

PREPARATION TIME: 4–5 minutes. COOKING TIME: 12 minutes.

1 1½–2 lb lobster
1 egg
¼ lb minced pork
1 tablespoon flour
2 tablespoons chopped
onion
1 clove garlic, chopped

2 teaspoons finely chopped
lemon-rind shavings
4 tablespoons 'broth' (see
pp.18–19)
1 tablespoon soya sauce
2 tablespoons sherry
2 tablespoons vegetable oil
1 tablespoon chopped parsley

Prepare lobster as in the preceding recipe. Place the segments meat-side up on a heatproof dish. Beat egg lightly. Combine with pork, flour and all the other ingredients except parsley. Mix together for 15 seconds. Spread the mixture thickly over each segment of lobster. Cook for 15 minutes in an oven preheated to 425 degrees. Sprinkle with chopped parsley and serve.

Prawns, Shrimps and Scallops

In China these seafoods or fresh-water products are, as often as not, used as flavourers – particularly in their dried state – rather than for food. Since they never require prolonged cooking, when cooked fresh, they are mostly stir-fried for a minute or two, either by themselves or in combination.

There is a belief in China that shell fish cooked in their shells are more flavourful. Since they are extremely tasty in any case, so long as they are fresh, we do not have to be biased in favour of cooking them in this manner. However, we shall start with one dish of prawns (or shrimps), which are cooked in their shells.

DRY-FRIED GIANT PRAWNS (OR SHRIMPS)

PREPARATION TIME: 4–6 minutes. COOKING TIME: 3–4 minutes.

6–8 large prawns (or shrimps)
2 stalks spring onion, cut into 1-inch segments
2 tablespoons 'broth' (see pp. 18–19)
1 tablespoon soya sauce
1 tablespoon sherry
1 teaspoon sugar
2 tablespoons vegetable oil
1 tablespoon chopped onion
1 clove garlic, chopped
½ teaspoon salt
1 tablespoon lard

Clean prawns thoroughly, remove dark and gritty parts, but do not remove the tail. Drain and dry. Mix spring onion in a bowl with 'broth', soya sauce, sherry and sugar.

Heat oil in frying-pan. Add chopped onion and garlic to stir-fry for ¼ minute over high heat. Add prawns, sprinkle with salt and stir-fry for 1¼ minutes. Pour in the 'broth'/soya sauce mixture, reserving the segments of spring onion. Stir the prawns in this sauce until it dries – which it should do in 1–2 minutes. Add lard and spring onion and stir-fry for ¼ minute. Serve on a well-heated dish; to be eaten immediately.

We Chinese normally eat this dish by inserting most of the prawn into the mouth (while holding onto the tail), and gradually biting and squeezing the end nearest the front teeth, so that the meat is squeezed out like toothpaste from a tube. This is accompanied by a sucking action which helps extract the meat, while increasing the sensation of sharp savouriness imparted by the near-dried sauce. This is a classical banquet dish.

QUICK-FRIED GIANT PRAWNS WITH TOMATOES

PREPARATION TIME: 3–4 minutes. COOKING TIME: 3–4 minutes.

Follow the preceding recipe. Skin 4 medium-sized tomatoes, and add them to the pan after the prawns have fried for ½ minute. Stir-fry them together for 1 minute over high heat, before adding the 'broth'/soya sauce mixture. Continue to stir-fry for 1 more minute. Here 1 tablespoon of tomato sauce may be added with 1 teaspoon of chilli sauce. Serve on a well-heated dish.

QUICK-FRIED SHRIMPS (OR SCALLOPS) WITH WINE SEDIMENT PASTE

PREPARATION TIME: 3–4 minutes. COOKING TIME: 2–3 minutes.

1 lb shrimp meat or 2 lb scallops	1 teaspoon salt
2 tablespoons lard	1 tablespoon chopped spring onion
2 teaspoons chopped lemon rind	2 tablespoons 'broth'
1 clove garlic, chopped	3 tablespoons wine sediment paste (see pp.21–2)

If using scallops, wash and shell them, remove tough root muscles, and slice each into 3–4 pieces.

Heat lard in a frying-pan. Add lemon rind, garlic, and salt. Stir-fry for ¼ minute, add spring onion, and shrimps or scallops. Continue to stir-fry for 1½ minutes. Add 'broth', and wine sediment paste, stir-fry for a further minute and serve on a well-heated dish.

QUICK-FRIED SHRIMPS (OR SCALLOPS) WITH MUSHROOMS IN GUNPOWDER SAUCE

PREPARATION TIME: 3–4 minutes. SOAKING TIME: 20 minutes (for dried mushrooms). COOKING TIME: 3–4 minutes.

1 lb shrimp meat or 2 lb scallops	(optional but preferable – see p.1)
6 large dried mushrooms	1 tablespoon sherry

¾ tablespoon cornflour,
blended in 2 tablespoons
water
4 tablespoons (mushroom)
water
1 teaspoon sugar
6 large mushrooms
(de-stemmed)

3 tablespoons lard
1 tablespoon chopped onion
1 clove garlic, chopped
1 teaspoon chopped lemon
rind
½ teaspoon salt
4 tablespoons gunpowder
sauce (see pp.19–20)

If using scallops, clean and prepare them as in previous
recipe. (If using dried mushrooms retain 4 tablespoons of the
water in which they are soaked). Mix sherry, cornflour mixture,
(mushroom) water and sugar in a bowl. Cut each piece of
mushroom into quarters.

Heat lard in a frying-pan. Stir-fry onion, garlic, lemon rind
and salt, for ½ minute. Add mushrooms and shrimps (or scallops) to fry together for 1 minute. Pour in the gunpowder
sauce and remaining (mushroom) water mixture, stir-fry
together for 2½ minutes and serve.

QUICK-FRIED CRYSTAL SHRIMPS

PREPARATION TIME: 2–3 minutes. MARINATING TIME: 10 minutes. COOKING TIME: 2–3 minutes.

1 lb shrimp meat (fresh or
frozen)
1 teaspoon salt
2 tablespoons sherry
2 tablespoons vegetable oil
1 tablespoon finely chopped
onion

1 clove garlic, crushed
2 tablespoons 'broth' (see
pp.18–19)
½ tablespoon cornflour,
blended in 2 tablespoons
water and 1 tablespoon
sherry

Sprinkle shrimps (should be thawed if frozen) with salt and
sherry. Leave for 10 minutes and drain away any liquid.

Heat oil in a frying-pan. Stir-fry onion and garlic over
moderate heat for 1 minute. Add the shrimps, spread them out,

and stir-fry gently for 1½ minutes. Pour in the 'broth' and stir-fry together with shrimps for ½ minute. Pour in the corn-flour mixture. Stir until the sauce thickens and is well mixed with the shrimps. Serve on a well-heated dish; to be eaten immediately.

QUICK-FRIED SHRIMPS WITH FU-YUNG SAUCE

PREPARATION TIME: 2–3 minutes. MARINATING TIME: 10 minutes. COOKING TIME: 3–4 minutes.

½ lb shrimp meat (fresh or frozen)
½ teaspoon salt
2 tablespoons sherry
2 tablespoons vegetable oil
1 tablespoon finely chopped onion
1 clove garlic, finely chopped

1½ tablespoons lard
1 4-inch segment of cucumber (well cleaned but not peeled)
2 tablespoons 'broth' (see pp.18–19)
6 tablespoons Fu-yung sauce (see pp.20–21)

Sprinkle shrimps with salt and sherry. Leave for 10 minutes and drain away any liquid. Dice cucumber into ¼-inch cubes.

Heat oil in a frying-pan. Add onion and garlic to stir-fry for ½ minute. Then add lard, shrimps and cucumber and continue to stir-fry for 1 minute. Pour in the 'broth', followed by the Fu-yung sauce. Stir together for ½ minute and serve.

STIR-FRIED 'PHOENIX' AND 'DRAGON'

PREPARATION TIME: 5–6 minutes. MARINATING TIME: 10 minutes. COOKING TIME: 5–6 minutes.

½ lb shrimp meat (fresh or frozen)
½ teaspoon salt

2 tablespoons sherry
1 breast of chicken (see note on p.86)

1 3-inch segment of cucumber (well cleaned but not peeled)
2 tablespoons vegetable oil
1 tablespoon finely chopped onion
1 clove garlic, crushed
2 tablespoons lard
½ cup button mushrooms
3 tablespoons wine sediment paste (see pp. 21–2)
1 teaspoon sugar
½ tablespoon soya sauce

Sprinkle shrimps with salt and sherry. Leave for 10 minutes and drain away any liquid. Dice chicken and cucumber into ¼-inch cubes.

Heat oil in a frying-pan. Stir-fry onion and garlic for 1 minute. Add shrimps and chicken. Stir-fry them together for 2 minutes. Remove with perforated spoon and put aside.

Melt lard in the pan; add diced cucumber and mushrooms. Stir-fry them together for 1 minute. Push them to one side of the pan. Add wine sediment paste into the centre of the pan. Mix it with the remaining oil. Return the shrimps and chicken to the pan. Stir-fry them together in the 'sauce' with the cucumber and mushrooms for 1 minute. Sprinkle with sugar and soya sauce. Continue to stir-fry for ½ minute, and serve.

This is something of a party dish, and is extremely flavoursome.

QUICK-FRIED SHRIMPS WITH BEAN-SPROUTS AND GROUND PORK

PREPARATION TIME: 3–4 minutes. COOKING TIME: 5–6 minutes.

2 tablespoons vegetable oil
1 tablespoon finely chopped onion
1 clove garlic, chopped
¼ lb minced pork
1 teaspoon salt
½ lb shrimp meat (fresh or frozen)
2 tablespoons lard
2 tablespoons spring onion, cut into 1-inch segments
½ lb (2 cups) bean-sprouts
1 tablespoon soya sauce
3 tablespoons 'broth' (see pp. 18–19)
½ teaspoon chilli sauce
3 tablespoons sherry

Heat oil in a frying-pan. Stir-fry onion and garlic for $\frac{1}{2}$ minute over high heat. Add pork and half the salt and stir-fry together for 2 minutes. Add shrimps and stir-fry together for 1 minute. Remove with perforated spoon and keep hot.

Melt lard in the pan; add the spring onion and bean-sprouts. Stir-fry over high heat for 1 minute. Return the shrimps and pork to the pan. Sprinkle with remaining salt, soya sauce, 'broth', chilli sauce and sherry. Continue to stir-fry over high heat for 1 minute, and serve.

QUICK-FRIED SHRIMPS WITH CELERY AND GROUND PORK

PREPARATION TIME: 3–4 minutes. COOKING TIME: 4–5 minutes.

Follow the preceding recipe, substituting celery (cut diagonally into $1\frac{1}{2}$-inch pieces) for bean-sprouts, but stir-fry for 1 minute longer before returning shrimps and pork to the pan for the final assembly frying.

Note: shrimps can, in fact, be cooked in the same manner with almost any kind of vegetable with similar success, except with hard vegetables, such as broccoli, cauliflower or asparagus, which will have to be parboiled for 3–4 minutes and drained before being added into the stir-frying. With soft vegetables, such as spinach or tomato, one has only to follow exactly the procedure of the above recipe. In this way a dozen or more recipes can be prepared by simply varying the combinations. In consequence, shrimps and prawns are among the most popular foods in Chinese cooking.

QUICK-FRIED SHRIMPS WITH SWEET PEPPERS IN HOT SAVOURY SAUCE

PREPARATION TIME: 2–3 minutes. COOKING TIME: 3–4 minutes.

2 red or green peppers
2 chilli peppers (if

unavailable, use 2 teaspoons
chilli sauce)

2 tablespoons vegetable oil
1 tablespoon finely chopped onion
1 clove garlic, chopped
½ lb shrimp meat (fresh or frozen)
1 tablespoon lard

½ teaspoon salt
1 tablespoon tomato sauce
2 tablespoons gunpowder sauce (see pp. 19–20)
1 teaspoon sugar
2 teaspoons vinegar
1 tablespoon sherry

Cut sweet peppers into pieces the size of shrimps and slice the chilli peppers into shreds, discarding pips.

Heat oil in a frying-pan. Stir-fry onion and garlic for ½ minute. Add shrimps and stir-fry for 1 minute. Remove and keep warm.

Add lard. When it has dissolved, add chilli pepper, and stir-fry over high heat for ¼ minute. Add sweet pepper and stir-fry together for 1½ minutes. Return the shrimps to the pan. Add all the other ingredients and continue to stir-fry together over high heat for 1 minute, serve, to be eaten immediately.

TOASTED SHRIMPS

This is a very similar dish to 'Toasted Fish' (see pp. 140–41).

PREPARATION TIME: 5–6 minutes. COOKING TIME: 2½–3 minutes.

¼–½ lb shrimp meat (fresh or frozen)
2 eggs
½ teaspoon salt
1 tablespoon chopped spring onion

1 tablespoon cornflour
4 slices of bread
¼ lb (2 cups) breadcrumbs
oil for deep-frying
parsley

Chop and mince the shrimp meat. Beat eggs for ¼ minute with rotary whisk in a bowl. Add ¼ of the beaten eggs to the minced shrimp, along with the salt, spring onion and cornflour. Mix well into a smooth paste. Trim away the crusts from the bread and cut each slice into quarters.

Spread the 'shrimp paste' heavily on each piece of bread. Spread half the breadcrumbs evenly on a tray. Dip the pieces of shrimp-pasted bread quickly in the remainder of the beaten egg and place on the breadcrumbs. Sprinkle heavily with remaining breadcrumbs. When all the pieces of shrimp-pasted bread have been crumbed, deep-fry them 4 at a time for 2½ minutes in very hot oil. Drain and arrange them neatly on a well-heated dish. Decorate each piece of shrimp toast with a pinch of chopped parsley, and serve. (An excellent item to serve as a canapé at a cocktail party.)

PHOENIX-TAIL SHRIMPS

PREPARATION TIME: 5–6 minutes. COOKING TIME: 7–8 minutes.

1 dozen fresh giant-size unshelled shrimps (or Pacific prawns)
½ teaspoon salt
1 egg

4 tablespoons flour
4 tablespoons water
1 tablespoon finely chopped onion
1 clove garlic, crushed

Clean and shell the shrimps, leaving the tails. Sprinkle and rub lightly with salt. Blend egg, flour, water, onion and garlic into a smooth batter. Dip the body of each shrimp into the batter.

Heat oil in a deep-fryer. When very hot place 4 shrimps at a time in a wire-basket and deep-fry for 2½ minutes. Serve to be eaten immediately by holding on to the shrimp tails, which should by now have turned quite pink or red. Best eaten dipped in salt-and-pepper mix (see p.22), (this is another fine dish for a cocktail party).

SHRIMP SCRAMBLED-OMELETTE

Whether this is an egg or a shrimp dish depends upon the relative quantity of the two materials used. In this case a preponderance of shrimps will be used.

PREPARATION TIME: 2–3 minutes. COOKING TIME: 2–3 minutes.

1 lb shrimp meat (fresh or frozen)	2 tablespoons chopped chives
1 teaspoon salt	4 tablespoons vegetable oil
3 eggs	pepper
	2 tablespoons sherry

Sprinkle and rub shrimps with half the salt. Beat eggs lightly with remaining salt and chives.

Heat oil in a frying-pan. Add shrimps and stir-fry gently for 1¼ minutes. Pour in the beaten egg. Tilt the pan so that the egg will flow evenly over the pan and shrimps. Keep the heat moderate. When the egg is three-quarters set, sprinkle with a liberal amount of pepper and the sherry. Stir and scramble the egg and shrimps lightly and serve on a well-heated dish; to be eaten immediately.

DRUNKEN SHRIMPS

MARINATING TIME: 3 hours. PREPARATION TIME: 10 minutes.

1 lb shrimp meat (must be very fresh)	1 tablespoon brandy (or rum)
2 teaspoons salt	freshly milled black pepper
2 cloves garlic, chopped	1 teaspoon chilli sauce
2 teaspoons finely chopped root ginger (or 1 tablespoon finely chopped lemon-rind shavings)	1 tablespoon soya sauce
	pepper
	2 teaspoons vegetable oil
	1 tablespoon chopped parsley
6 tablespoons sherry	1 tablespoon chopped chives

Sprinkle and rub shrimps with salt, garlic, ginger and sherry. Place in a refrigerator to marinate for 3 hours.

Drain away the marinade completely. Sprinkle with brandy, chilli sauce, soya sauce, pepper and oil, and work into the shrimps with fingers. Arrange nicely on dish. Sprinkle with chopped parsley and chives and serve. (An excellent item for an hors d'oeuvre.)

Oysters

Oysters are never eaten raw in China, as we consider this a barbarous and dangerous practice. In Chinese cooking they are usually deep-fried, quick-fried or pre-fried and 'assembled' with other food materials to enhance and vary their flavours. Unlike shrimps, oysters are a purely coastal delicacy. The following are some of the ways they are usually prepared and cooked.

DEEP-FRIED OYSTERS

PREPARATION TIME: 8–10 minutes. MARINATING TIME: 15 minutes. COOKING TIME: 7–8 minutes.

2 dozen oysters
1½ teaspoons salt
pepper
1 medium size onion, finely chopped

3 tablespoons sherry
oil for deep-frying
1 tablespoon chopped chives

For Batter:

1 egg
6 tablespoons flour

1 tablespoon self-raising flour
6 tablespoons water

Shell oysters. Sprinkle with salt, pepper, chopped onion and sherry. Season for 15 minutes, and discard marinade.

Beat egg lightly. Blend with flour and water into a light batter.

Heat oil in the deep-fryer. When very hot, dip oysters in batter, and deep-fry 5–6 at a time for 2 minutes. Drain on paper towels. Arrange on a well-heated dish, sprinkle with chopped chives and serve.

DEEP-FRIED OYSTERS IN WINE SEDIMENT PASTE

Follow the preceding recipe. When all the oysters have been deep-fried, heat 4 tablespoons wine sediment paste (see page 32) and 1½ tablespoons lard in a frying-pan. When hot stir them together for ¼ minute. Add all the deep-fried oysters, sprinkle with chives, turn them in the sauce for ¾ minute and serve.

BARBECUED (OR ROAST) OYSTERS

In some parts of coastal China (such as Fukien) oysters are grown in beds stuck with forests of bamboo sticks. When in season they are harvested by simply pulling up the sticks, around which oysters have grown or stuck in clusters. These 'sticks' of oysters are then simply turned around and around over a charcoal brazier, becoming 'barbecued oysters'. As the oysters are cooked their shells pop open. For convenience in the West – where your oysters do not grow on sticks – it is easiest to roast them.

PREPARATION TIME: 6–8 minutes. COOKING TIME: 10–12 minutes.

2 dozen oysters

For Dips:

Soya-tomato dip (2 tablespoons soya sauce mixed with 2 tablespoons tomato sauce).
Soya-chilli dip (3 tablespoons soya sauce with 2 tablespoons chilli sauce).
Soya-sherry-garlic dip (2 tablespoons soya sauce, with 2 tablespoons sherry and 1 clove chopped garlic).
Lemon juice (squeeze from fresh lemon).
Soya-vinegar-ginger dip (2 tablespoons each of soya sauce

and vinegar, with two teaspoons chopped fresh ginger or dried ginger).

Clean oysters thoroughly and arrange them on a roasting-pan or large flat heatproof dish in a single layer. Place the pan or dish in an oven, preheated to 475 degrees, for 10–12 minutes.

By that time most of the oysters, having been cooked in their own juice, will have popped open. The dish or pan is then brought directly to the dining-table where each diner, equipped with a spoon and fork, will take one oyster at a time and eat it after first dabbing it into various dips. When served in such a way, people (including the author) have been known to consume a hundred oysters at one sitting without ill effect!

QUICK-FRIED OYSTERS WITH GROUND PORK AND MUSHROOMS

PREPARATION TIME: 6–8 minutes. SOAKING TIME: 20 minutes (for dried mushrooms). COOKING TIME: 6–8 minutes.

6 dried mushrooms (optional but preferable – see p.1)
2 tablespoons vegetable oil
1 tablespoon finely chopped onion
1 clove garlic, chopped
½ teaspoon salt
1 dozen oysters (shelled)
1 tablespoon lard

¼ lb minced pork
6 mushrooms (medium or large, de-stemmed)
1½ tablespoons soya sauce
2 tablespoons sherry
1 teaspoon chilli sauce
4 tablespoons (mushroom) water

If using dried mushrooms, retain 4 tablespoons of the water in which they are soaked. Heat oil in a frying-pan. Add onion, garlic and salt. Stir-fry for ½ minute. Pour in the oysters and stir-fry for 1 minute. Remove with perforated spoon and keep warm.

Add lard and pork to the pan. Stir-fry pork for 2 minutes. Tip in the mushrooms. Stir-fry them together with pork for another 1½ minutes. Pour in the soya sauce, sherry, chilli sauce and (mushroom) water. Return the oysters to the pan for ¾ minute of assembly frying. Serve to be eaten immediately.

QUICK-FRIED OYSTERS WITH PORK AND VEGETABLES

PREPARATION TIME: 6–8 minutes. COOKING TIME: 6–8 minutes. PARBOILING: 3 minutes.

Oysters, like shrimps, can be cooked with pork and most types of vegetables (such as broccoli, cauliflower, greens, spinach or celery) in the same manner as with mushrooms in the previous recipe. With fresh vegetables, as with fresh mushrooms, no soaking is required; with the hard vegetables, 3–5 minutes of parboiling might be required, and, of course, they will have to be cut into 1-inch slices or broken into individual branches before being added to the pan.

Vegetables

Chinese vegetable dishes are exceptionally tasty, mainly because the cross-blending of flavours gives them great richness of taste without detracting from their freshness. As we have already seen in previous chapters, a majority of meat and poultry dishes are, in fact, mixed dishes, cooked with a large percentage of vegetables. Except for the pure vegetarian dishes, most Chinese vegetable dishes are cooked with meat broths or contain some element of meat. In addition, vegetables are often made more piquant by cooking them with dried, salted or pickled vegetables, as well as those which are strong-flavoured. These consist of such things as pickles, chutneys, capers, root ginger (or dried ginger, but not powdered), garlic, onion and dried mushrooms. Such ingredients are often cooked in oil first, and then the bulk vegetables are added to cook in the flavour-impregnated oil.

Vegetable dishes are essential for giving balance to a meal. There should be at least one vegetable dish to every three meat, fish, poultry or mixed dish. Since vegetables do not usually require prolonged cooking, the majority of vegetable dishes are produced in a matter of minutes which means that they should fall naturally into the scope of quick and easy chinese cooking. Dishes are classified in China as vegetable dishes if they have a preponderance of vegetables.

Portions: all the following recipes are meant for 4–6 people, when served with 1 meat dish, rice, and 1 or 2 other dishes.

PLAIN FRIED SPINACH

PREPARATION TIME: 2–3 minutes. COOKING TIME: 4–5 minutes.

1 lb spinach
4 tablespoons vegetable oil
2 tablespoons finely chopped onion
1 clove garlic, chopped
½ tablespoon finely chopped ginger root (or 1 teaspoon

finely chopped lemon-rind shavings)
1 tablespoon chopped mixed pickles
1 teaspoon salt
4 tablespoons gunpowder sauce (see pp. 19–20)
2 teaspoons sugar

Clean and drain spinach thoroughly, discarding coarser parts.

Heat oil in a large saucepan. Add onion, garlic, ginger, pickles. Stir-fry over high heat for ½ minute and add spinach and salt. Turn the vegetables in the hot, flavour-impregnated oil for 1½ minutes. Add gunpowder sauce and sugar, and continue to stir-fry over high heat for 2–2½ minutes and serve.

STIR-FRIED SPINACH WITH SHRIMPS

PREPARATION TIME: 2–3 minutes. COOKING TIME: 4–5 minutes.

Follow the preceding recipe, adding 4–6 tablespoons fresh shrimps a fraction of a moment before adding the spinach into the pan for the stir-fry; thus the shrimp taste will impregnate the oil, which will in turn impregnate the spinach.

SPINACH AND NOODLES GARNISHED WITH SHREDDED HAM

The preceding two dishes are meant as one of three or four dishes to be served at a full sit-down meal, but the following recipe should make a highly nutritious but economical dish for a self-contained snack (for three):

PREPARATION TIME: 3–4 minutes. COOKING TIME: 5–6 minutes. PARBOILING: 5–6 minutes for noodles or vermicelli (17–18 for spaghetti).

Proceed as in either of the two previous recipes. Meanwhile, parboil 1 lb of noodles, vermicelli or spaghetti, and shred 3 slices of ham (about 3–4 oz or half a cup when shredded). When the spinach has cooked in the saucepan, tip in the noodles, 2 tablespoons butter and 6 tablespoons gunpowder sauce. Stir and toss over low heat until the noodles and spinach are well mixed. Pour the spinach/noodles out on a large well-heated dish (or into 3 bowls), garnish with shredded ham and serve.

QUICK-FRIED SPINACH WITH RED-COOKED MEAT

(*Either pork or beef can be used*)

PREPARATION TIME: 2–3 minutes. COOKING TIME: 3–4 minutes.

Follow the above recipe. When the spinach is ready, use it as the bed in a round or oval deep-sided dish. Place 1–1½ lb Red-cooked Beef or Pork (see pages 78 or 57–8) on top, into the centre of the dish. The contrast between the glistening green of spinach and the rich brown of the beef or pork make it a very attractive dish.

QUICK-FRIED SPINACH WITH PORK AND MUSHROOMS

PREPARATION TIME: 4–5 minutes. COOKING TIME: 5–6 minutes.

The basic method employed here is to stir-fry the spinach and pork-and-mushrooms separately, and combine them together in an assembly frying for 1 minute before serving.

Cook the spinach as in the recipe for Plain Fried Spinach.

After it is cooked, cover and keep warm. Slice $\frac{1}{4}$ lb pork into thin 2-inch × 1-inch pieces. Stir-fry it in 2 tablespoons oil, together with 6–8 mushrooms (de-stemmed) and 2 table-spoons gunpowder sauce for 3 minutes. Add this mixture to the spinach for a final assembly frying, along with 2 tablespoons of sherry and a pinch of salt and pepper. (If dried mushrooms are used, some 3–4 tablespoons of mushroom water derived from soaking the dried mushrooms for 20–30 minutes in hot water may also be added at this point.)

RED-COOKED CABBAGE

PREPARATION TIME: 2–3 minutes. COOKING TIME: 8–9 minutes.

1 2–3 lb medium-sized cabbage (savoy or Chinese celery-cabbage)
3 tablespoons vegetable oil
1 medium-sized onion, chopped
1 clove garlic, chopped
1 slice root ginger (or $\frac{1}{2}$

tablespoon finely chopped lemon-rind shavings)
$\frac{1}{2}$ teaspoon salt
2 teaspoons sugar
1 teaspoon chilli sauce
6 tablespoons gunpowder sauce (see pp. 19–20)
2 tablespoons sherry

Chop cabbage into 2-inch × 1-inch pieces, discarding coarser leaves and root.

Heat oil in a saucepan. Add onion and garlic. Stir-fry for $\frac{1}{2}$ minute; add all the cabbage and the butter. Sprinkle with salt, turn and stir the cabbage so that it is all well lubricated with oil.

After 2 minutes of slow stir-frying, add sugar, chilli sauce, gunpowder sauce and sherry. Continue to stir-fry for 1 minute. Lower the heat to fairly low and close the lid of the saucepan. Allow the contents to cook under cover for 4–5 minutes. Open the lid, give the cabbage a last stir, and serve in a bowl or large deep-sided dish.

In a more elaborate version of this dish, half a dozen soaked dried mushrooms (together with 3–4 tablespoons of mush-

room water) are added just before the braising, which is prolonged by 1 minute.

WHITE-COOKED CABBAGE

PREPARATION TIME: 2–3 minutes. COOKING TIME: 8–10 minutes.

Prepare the cabbage, and cook it with the same initial ingredients as in the previous recipe, but in the second stage of the
cooking, substitute 6 tablespoons 'broth' (see pp.18–19), 4
tablespoons Fu-yung sauce (see pp.20–21) and 1 teaspoon salt
for gunpowder sauce.

Allow the cabbage mixture to cook under cover over low–
moderate heat for 6–7 minutes; and wind up by sprinkling the
cabbage with pepper and 2 additional tablespoons sherry for a
final ½ minute stir-fry before serving in a bowl or deep-sided
dish.

For a slightly more elaborate dish, 2–3 tablespoons of
minced or chopped ham are used to sprinkle as garnish on the
cabbage.

The above two dishes are classical ways of cooking Chinese
cabbage, and are very popular both among rich and poor. The
majority of Westerners have also found them extremely appealing. Like many Chinese vegetable dishes they can be eaten
on their own or used as 'starters', although they are normally
served to balance and complement meat and mixed dishes.

CABBAGE WITH MEAT-TOPPED OR
SHRIMP-TOPPED NOODLES

TIME: Indicated during the recipe.

For quick meals, which are self-contained and highly satisfac-
tory, half a pint of boiled egg-noodles can be added to either of
the above two dishes, and topped with a cup or two of red-
cooked beef (see p.78), red-cooked pork (see pp.57–8), or any
of the shrimp dishes from the preceding chapter.

BEAN-SPROUTS QUICK-FRIED WITH SHREDDED PORK

PREPARATION TIME: 2–3 minutes. COOKING TIME: 4½ minutes.

¼ lb lean pork
3 tablespoons vegetable oil
1 tablespoon finely chopped onion
1 clove garlic, chopped
1 teaspoon salt

1 lb bean-sprouts
1½ tablespoons soya sauce
3 tablespoons 'broth' (see pp.18–19)
1 tablespoon vinegar

Shred pork into thin strips. Heat oil in a frying-pan and stir-fry onion, garlic, pork and salt together for 1½ minutes over high heat. Add the bean-sprouts and stir-fry for 1½ minutes. Pour in the soya sauce, 'broth' and vinegar and continue to stir-fry for 1½ minutes; serve, to be eaten immediately.

SLICED CELERY QUICK-FRIED WITH SHREDDED PORK

PREPARATION TIME: 2–3 minutes. COOKING TIME: 5½ minutes.

Follow the preceding recipe, substituting 1 lb (approximately 2½ cups) sliced celery (sliced diagonally to ¼-inch thickness) for bean-sprouts. Also add 4 tablespoons gunpowder sauce instead of soya sauce, and extend the final stages of stir-frying by 1 minute, thus extending the overall cooking time to 5½ minutes. This will help in softening the celery, which is a harder vegetable than bean-sprouts.

QUICK-FRIED CELERY (OR CABBAGE) IN SWEET AND SOUR SAUCE

PREPARATION TIME: 2–3 minutes. COOKING TIME: 4–5 minutes.

3 cups cabbage *or* celery
3 tablespoons vegetable oil

1 tablespoon onion, finely chopped

1 clove garlic, chopped
1 teaspoon salt
4–6 tablespoons sweet and

sour sauce (see p.21)
3 tablespoons 'broth' (see
pp.18–19)

Slice cabbage in 1½-inch × ¾-inch pieces *or* slice celery diagonally. Heat oil in a saucepan or large frying-pan. Add onion, garlic and salt, and stir-fry together for 2 minutes over high heat. Add cabbage and continue to stir-fry for 5 minutes. Add sweet and sour sauce and 'broth'; stir-fry for a further 2 minutes over high heat, and serve. This dish can be eaten hot or cold.

RED- OR WHITE-COOKED CELERY

PREPARATION TIME: 2–3 minutes. COOKING TIME: 10–11 minutes.

In Chinese cooking celery is considered as a similar type of vegetable as cabbage (the Chinese variety has a similar texture). It can, therefore, be red-cooked or white-cooked in much the same manner as cabbage, by simply repeating the recipes for Red-cooked Cabbage and White-cooked cabbage – except that with celery a minute or two longer cooking will be required, and the addition of a couple of tablespoons of soaked dried mushrooms (shredded) and soaked dried shrimps (if available) will be an asset. These should be added when the bulk of the vegetables are added.

QUICK-FRIED WHITE-BRAISED CAULIFLOWER

PREPARATION TIME: 1–2 minutes. COOKING TIME: 5–6 minutes.

1 large cauliflower
3 tablespoons vegetable oil
1 clove garlic, crushed
1 onion, finely chopped
1 teaspoon salt

pepper
¼ cup 'broth' (see pp.18–19)
2 tablespoons sherry
2 tablespoons chopped ham
(or 1 teaspoon paprika)

Cut the cauliflower into individual branches or flowerlets, discarding root and coarse parts.

Heat oil in a saucepan and stir-fry garlic and onion over high heat for $\frac{1}{4}$ minute. Add cauliflower, sprinkle with salt and pepper and turn in the hot oil for 2 minutes. Pour in 'broth' and sherry. Turn the vegetables over once in the sauce, and close the lid of the saucepan. Cook under cover for $3\frac{1}{2}$ minutes over low heat. Pour the cauliflower and sauce into a deep-sided dish. Sprinkle with chopped ham or paprika and serve.

QUICK-FRIED HOT-BRAISED BROCCOLI TOPPED WITH CRAB-MEAT

PREPARATION TIME: 2–3 minutes. COOKING TIME: 5–6 minutes.

For garnish:

4–5 tablespoons crab-meat $\frac{1}{2}$ tablespoon chopped spring
$1\frac{1}{2}$ tablespoons oil   onion
1 clove garlic, crushed

Cook broccoli in the same way as the cauliflower in the previous recipe, omitting the garlic and adding 1 teaspoon chilli sauce along with the 'broth'. Instead of the chopped ham or paprika garnish, the crab-meat is fried in oil with garlic and spring onion for 1 minute over high heat.

QUICK-FRIED BROCCOLI OR CAULIFLOWER IN FU-YUNG SAUCE

PREPARATION TIME: 2–3 minutes. COOKING TIME: 6–7 minutes.

Follow the directions for Quick-fried White-braised Cauliflower but add 6 tablespoons Fu-yung sauce (see pp.20–21) for $\frac{3}{4}$ minute slow stir-frying or folding in, before garnishing with ham or crab-meat.

QUICK-FRIED BRAISED LETTUCE

PREPARATION TIME: 2 minutes. COOKING TIME: 5 minutes.

2 lettuces (about ¾–1 lb)
2 tablespoons butter
1 teaspoon salt
2 tablespoons shredded ham
8 tablespoons (½ cup) 'broth'
(see pp. 18–19)

1 tablespoon cornflour,
blended with 2 tablespoons
water and 2 tablespoons
sherry

Wash and cut off the roots of the lettuces, separating the full-length leaves.

Heat butter in a frying-pan. When it has melted, turn the lettuce in the butter for 2½ minutes over moderate heat; sprinkle with salt. Add chopped ham and 'broth'. Leave it to cook for 2 minutes, turning it over a couple of times. Pour in the cornflour/water/sherry mixture. Turn the lettuce over a few more times in the thickened sauce, which should now be translucent. Serve, to be eaten immediately; to accompany browner and richer dishes.

QUICK-FRIED LEEKS OR SWEET PEPPER WITH SHREDDED BEEF

PREPARATION TIME: 3–4 minutes. COOKING TIME: 5–6 minutes.

Both leeks and sweet peppers are strong-flavoured vegetables. They are seldom cooked and eaten on their own. More often than not they are cooked together with a small amount of strong-flavoured meat, such as beef or lamb.

3 medium-sized red or
green peppers, or ¾ lb leeks
2 tablespoons butter
1 teaspoon salt

1 tablespoon vegetable oil
¼ lb beef (shredded into thin
strips)
1 clove garlic, chopped

1 teaspoon sugar
1 tablespoon soya sauce
3 tablespoons 'broth' (see pp.18–19)

½ teaspoon chilli sauce
1 tablespoon sherry

Clean and cut leeks or peppers into approximately 1½-inch × ¾-inch pieces.

Heat butter in a large frying-pan. Add leek or pepper, sprinkle with salt, and stir-fry for 1½ minutes over moderate heat. Remove from heat. Heat oil in a small frying-pan. Add shredded beef, garlic, sugar and soya sauce; stir-fry over moderate heat for 1 minute. Tip the beef into the large frying-pan with 'broth', chilli sauce and sherry. Turn and stir-fry with leek or pepper over high heat for 1¼ minutes. Serve, to be eaten immediately.

CASSEROLE OF CABBAGE AND BRUSSELS SPROUTS WITH PIG'S TROTTERS

PREPARATION TIME: 2–3 minutes. COOKING TIME: 3 hours.

2 pairs of pig's trotters (approximately 1½–2 lb)
1 cabbage (approximately 1½–2 lb)
2 teaspoons salt
½ pint 'broth' (see pp.18–19)

½ cup sherry
1 chicken stock cube
2 tablespoons chopped onion
1 lb brussels sprouts (quartered and coarse leaves discarded)

Clean and parboil the trotters for 3 minutes. Drain and place at the bottom of a large casserole. Remove root of cabbage and cut vertically into 8 pieces. Place them over and around the trotters. Sprinkle with salt and 2 pints water. Place the casserole in an oven preheated to 425 degrees. Cook for 10 minutes and reduce to 325 degrees. Leave to cook for 2 hours under cover. Open the lid, add 'broth', sherry, stock cube, and the sprouts. Replace the lid of the casserole and return it to the oven for another hour at 325 degrees. Serve in the casserole.

This semi-soup dish, with a large quantity of vegetables, is a boon to eat with rice. It is meant to remain on the table so diners can help themselves from it throughout the meal. The liquid is often drunk as soup after the vegetables have been consumed.

CASSEROLE OF CABBAGE AND BRUSSELS SPROUTS WITH SQUABS

PREPARATION TIME: 3–4 minutes. COOKING TIME: 2 hours.

Follow the preceding recipe, substituting squabs for trotters, red wine for sherry and 2 tablespoons soya sauce for 'broth'. Reduce the initial cooking time by 1 hour.

The meat of the squab is usually eaten after the vegetables and the soup.

CASSEROLE OF LEEKS AND CABBAGE WITH LAMB CHOPS

PREPARATION TIME: 3–4 minutes. COOKING TIME: 2 hours.

1½ lb lamb chops
1 clove garlic, crushed
1½ lb (approx 3–4 cups) cabbage cut into 2-inch × ½-inch pieces

1 lb leeks cut into 2-inch segments
2 teaspoons salt
1 cup 'broth' (see pp.18–19)
1 cup sherry
2 tablespoons soya sauce

Place the lamb chops at the bottom of a casserole. Add garlic and cover with cabbage and leeks. Pour in ½ pint water and sprinkle with salt. Place in oven at 425 degrees for 15 minutes and reduce to 350 degrees for 1 hour. Add 'broth', sherry and adjust seasoning with soya sauce. Cook for another ¾ hour and serve in the casserole.

This is another favourite semi-soup dish which is eaten throughout the meal, starting with the vegetables and ending by drinking the soup and eating all the meat from the chops, which should be very tender.

STEAMED 'VEGETABLE BOWL'

PREPARATION TIME: 7–8 minutes. SOAKING TIME: 20 minutes (for dried mushrooms). COOKING TIME: 45 minutes.

½ marrow (about 2 lb)
3 hearts of spring greens
¼ small cabbage
¼ lb spinach
1 bundle watercress
2 teaspoons salt
1 pint 'broth' (see pp.18–19)
2 tablespoons butter

6 large mushrooms (de-stemmed)
6 dried mushrooms (optional but desirable – see p.1)
1½ tablespoons soya sauce
1 teaspoon sugar
4 tablespoons sherry

This dish should only be attempted if you have a steamer or large boiler in which a very large deep-sided dish, containing the vegetables, can be conveniently placed on a rack or raised platform, and 1½–2 inches of water in the boiler can be kept at a rolling boil without splashing into the dish containing the vegetables.

Cut the marrow into 4-inch × 2-inch pieces after removing the skin and seeds. Cut each heart of spring green vertically into twos. Stand the marrow pieces and hearts of green around the wall of the deep-sided dish. Fill up the well in the middle with chopped cabbage (2-inch × 1-inch pieces), spinach which has been thoroughly cleaned, and watercress (with white roots removed). Sprinkle with salt and pour in the 'broth'.

Heat butter in a frying-pan. When it has melted, add the mushrooms and stir-fry for 1 minute. Add soya sauce and sugar, and stir-fry for a further 1 minute. Place the mushrooms on top of the watercress at the centre of the vegetable dish. Pour the remaining butter and gravy from the pan over the mushrooms. Place the dish in the steamer, or on a raised platform in the cauldron or boiler, and steam vigorously for ½ hour. Add sherry, adjust the seasoning, continue to steam for 15 minutes more and bring the dish directly from the steamer to serve on the table.

CHINESE SALAD

PREPARATION TIME: 5–6 minutes.

A Chinese salad differs from the average western salad only in the composition of the dressing. We use soya sauce, concentrated 'broth', sesame oil, root ginger and sherry. Sesame oil is used only for flavouring, so only a very small amount is used. Root ginger has a very distinctive taste to contribute but, if not available, use chopped lemon-rind shavings. Where available also use chopped coriander leaves, which contribute a memorable and unmistakable flavour.

For Dressing:

3 tablespoons soya sauce
½ teaspoon salt
4 tablespoons concentrated 'broth' (melt ¼ chicken stock cube in 4 tablespoons 'broth' – see pp.18–19)
1 teaspoon chopped root ginger (or 2 teaspoons chopped lemon rind)
1 clove garlic, chopped
2 tablespoons sherry

2 tablespoons wine vinegar
½ teaspoon chilli sauce
2 teaspoons sugar
pepper
4 tablespoons salad oil
1 teaspoon sesame oil (or 2 teaspoons peanut oil)
2 teaspoons chopped chives
1 tablespoon chopped coriander (if available)

Combine the above ingredients into a dressing.

The 'dressing' can be applied to salads or combinations of raw vegetables, such as:

Lettuce, shredded cabbage, sliced cucumber, celery, celeriac, carrots, radishes, tomatoes, chicory, etc. Some hard vegetables, such as cauliflower and broccoli, can also be used successfully in salads if parboiled for 3–4 minutes first.

The dressing from the above ingredients should be sufficient for a very large bowl of vegetables (1–2 lb). The presence of sesame oil, soya sauce, ginger and concentrated 'broth' gives this salad a very distinctive and appealing flavour.

Sweets

There are few sweets in China which compare with the more sophisticated range of desserts in the west. However, there are some Chinese sweets which, because of their difference in approach and concept, are intriguing and appealing and do not require too elaborate a process to prepare.

Portions: all the following recipes are meant to serve 4–6 people.

Almond Curd

Chinese almond curd is a jelly made out of finely ground almonds with milk, sweetened water and gelatine (or *agar agar*). When set, the jelly is cut into ½-inch cubes or diamond shapes, and served in syrup. The significant contribution here is the introduction of a nutty flavour to sweetened fruit dishes.

Walnuts, chestnuts or even peanuts can also be prepared in this manner. When the powdered nuts have been jellied and cut into cubes and diamonds, they can be served with different combinations of fruits to give fruit salads a new dimension in texture and flavour.

ALMOND CURD

PREPARATION TIME: 7–8 minutes. COOKING TIME: 3–4 minutes.
SETTING: 1–2 hours.

½ lb almond meat
2 cups water
4 tablespoons sugar
1 cup evaporated milk

1–1½ envelopes gelatine
(dissolve in ½ cup water)
½ teaspoon almond extract

Grind and blend almonds into a smooth paste in a mixer, in 2 lots (each lot with 1 cup of water). Filter through a double cheese-cloth into a bowl. Add sugar; stir to dissolve.

Heat evaporated milk in a saucepan. Add almond mixture and stir in the dissolved gelatine. Add almond extract. Stir slowly until ingredients are well blended.

Pour the mixture into a shallow dish to cool. When cool place in a refrigerator to set. When the curd or jelly is well set, cut it into ½-inch cubes or diamond shapes. Served with any combination of fruit cocktail.

Glazed Fruits

The best known of these glazed fruits is Glazed Apple, which in essence consists of cut pieces of apple dipped into hot molten sugar, and then momentarily dipped into a bowl of ice water to chill the molten sugar-coating into a brittle crust. The crust cracks readily when bitten into, providing both an interesting sensation and a sharp taste of sweetness, which is especially welcomed after a savoury meal. In Peking the dish is called Silk-thread Apples because of the long glass-like threads the apples draw when removed from the molten sugar in which they have been immersed.

GLAZED SILK-THREAD APPLES

PREPARATION TIME: 7–8 minutes. COOKING TIME: 9–10 minutes.

3–4 apples

For Batter:

1 egg
½ cup water

1 cup flour
oil for deep-frying

For Glazing Syrup:

4 tablespoons sugar
1 tablespoon honey

4 tablespoons peanut oil

Core the apples and cut each into 8 pieces. Mix the ingredients for batter into a smooth mixture. Dip apple into batter, divide into 3 lots and deep-fry each lot for 2½ minutes. Drain on paper towels.

Heat the peanut oil in a saucepan; add the sugar and honey. Stir and heat gently until ingredients have formed into a thick consistent syrup. Dip the apples in the syrup. Pull them out quickly and give them a quick dip in a large bowl of ice-water. Remove immediately and let them drain on each individual diner's plate.

What can be done with apples here can also be done with other fruits of similar texture, such as peaches, pears or even bananas, which are often prepared in this manner.

STEAMED PEARS

Steamed Pears are another generic form of Chinese hot fruit dessert. What can be done with pears can also be done with other fruits of similar shape, size and texture, such as apples and peaches.

PREPARATION TIME: 8–10 minutes. COOKING TIME: 30–35 minutes. CHILLING: 2 hours.

6 pears
6 teaspoons Kirsch, or any
suitable liqueur (i.e. fruit
brandies, Crème de Menthe)

3 tablespoons castor sugar
1 pint of sugar water (4
tablespoons sugar dissolved
in 1 pint water)

Peel the pears neatly, except for the part immediately surrounding the stalk (retain stalk). Slice ¼ inch off the bottoms so that they will stand or sit firmly. Arrange the 6 pears upright on a deep-sided heatproof dish. Pour in the sugar water. Place the dish in a steamer, or on a raised platform mounted in a large boiler. Steam steadily for 30–35 minutes. Remove the dish from the boiler. Sprinkle the pears with castor sugar and liqueur. Allow them to cool for 10–15 minutes and then place the dish in a refrigerator to chill for 2 hours.

When serving divide the pears into 6 individual serving bowls or cups. Pour some of the syrup over each of the pears.

In the more elaborate versions – if time is of little consideration – the ½-inch top of each pear is cut off (to form a lid with the stalk attached) and the fruit is carefully cored half-way through. The cavity of the core is then filled with cinnamon-flavoured honey, nuts, other fruits or whatever you like. The pears are then steamed with 'lids' on. When ready the pears can be painted with artificial food-colouring before sprinkling with castor sugar and liqueur.

MINIATURE ICE-MOUNTAINS

Another Chinese custom in serving peeled fruits is to sprinkle or dip them in sugar. In this case, the fruit is first peeled and chopped to somewhat larger size than normally used in fruit salads or cocktails. Next, it is covered with a pile of chipped ice, then sprinkled with coloured sugar and served.

PREPARATION TIME: 10–15 minutes.

4–6 individual bowls fruit salad (coarsely chopped)
2 cups of chipped ice (as dry as possible)

4–6 tablespoons multi-coloured 'Rainbow' sugar
4–6 teaspoons liqueur (Kirsch, cherry brandy, Crème de Menthe, etc)

Place the fruit salad in the refrigerator to chill for one hour. Prepare the chipped ice ten minutes before serving. Place in deep-freezer to chill and dry.

When ready to serve, pile ¼ cup of chipped ice on top of the centre of each bowl of fruit salad, sprinkle with liqueur and multi-coloured sugar and serve.

Chipped ice so treated has the quality of water-ice, and the touch of liqueur provides just that additional refreshing impact. This dessert follows in a Chinese tradition, but is served in a way which is more suitable to western usage. In Peking it is served on a large dish, using chipped ice as bed, and with individual dishes of sugar strategically placed as dips. The pieces of fruit are picked up, dipped and eaten with chopsticks.

Index

Cookery and Home Management